Foreign Affairs
The Best of 2017

Foreign Affairs December 2017

Our Top Picks from Print and Web

TABLE OF CONTENTS

BEST OF PRINT

The Opening of the North Korean Mind

Pyongyang Versus the Digital Underground

Jieun Baek

North Korean leader Kim Jong Un at a fish farm, in an undated photo released by North Korean state media in May 2015.

On a cold, clear night in September 2014, a man I'll call Ahn walked up to the edge of the Tumen River on the Chinese side of the heavily guarded border between China and North Korea. At its narrowest points, the Tumen measures a little over 150 feet wide, and Ahn could easily see the North Korean side from where he stood. In two bags, he was carrying 100 USB drives filled with films, television shows, music, and e-books from around the world.

Almost anywhere else, such material would be considered completely innocuous. At this border, however, it constitutes highly illicit, dangerous contraband. In the totalitarian state of North Korea, citizens are allowed to see and hear only those media products created or sanctioned by the government. Pyongyang considers foreign information of any kind a threat and expends great effort keeping it out. The regime's primary fear is that exposure to words, images, and sounds from the outside world could make North Koreans disillusioned with the state of affairs in their own country, which could lead them to desire—or even demand—change.

Ahn is a defector who escaped from North Korea in 2004 and now lives in the South Korean capital, Seoul, where he runs a nongovernmental organization that sends information into North Korea. He is one of the dozens of defectors from North Korea whom I have interviewed in the past ten years. Defectors' testimony is not always reliable, nor is it enough to piece together an accurate portrait of life inside the opaque and secretive country. But when combined with other information, defectors' stories offer invaluable insights.

At the edge of the river that night, Ahn knew precisely what to do; he had made this kind of trip to the border many times before. With his senses on high alert, he scanned the area for guards. Once he felt certain that he wasn't being watched, he placed his USB drives into a plastic bin, which he wrapped in a thick plastic bag. He then tied the package to a sturdy wire, grabbed one end, and hurled the bin into the air. It landed in the water, close to the North Korean bank of the river. There, a North Korean man whom I will call Ku stealthily waded in and grabbed the bin.

Of the two men, Ku had the far more dangerous job: taking the goods into North Korea. Ahn's organization was paying him the equivalent of approximately $100 to retrieve the USB drives, a sizable fee that would allow Ku to provide for his household for a month or two. But Ku was taking a huge risk: if North Korean border guards caught him, he could be beaten, sent to a prison camp, or even executed. Ku climbed out of the river and shed his incriminating wet clothes. He changed into a dry outfit and made his way back into the city where he lives. (I'm withholding the location at the request of Ahn's organization.) There, Ku sold each drive for about $1 on the black market to fellow citizens eager to get a glimpse of life on the outside.

Although North Korea is often referred to as "the hermit kingdom," over the past two decades, many cracks have appeared in the wall that the state has built around its people. Rudimentary media-smuggling operations such as Ahn's have helped North Koreans learn more about their country and the outside world, often at great risk to themselves.

Despite the threat of punishment by North Korea's brutal security forces, distributing foreign information has become a profitable business in North Korea. This is partly due to the ways in which the country's traditionally closed economy has changed in the past 20 years. From 1994 until 1998, an extraordinary famine swept North Korea, killing hundreds of thousands—perhaps even millions—of people. In response to its failure to feed its people, the government allowed small markets known as jangmadang to open so that people could buy basic goods from one another or barter.

The jangmadang represented a rudimentary form of capitalism profoundly at odds with the hard-line communism and state control of the economy that the government had enforced for decades. But when the famine finally subsided, the regime decided to continue tolerating most of the jangmadang, possibly out of a recognition that the state alone could not reliably provide for the majority of its people.

Since then, the small, informal markets have evolved into sophisticated, large-scale operations, some of which feature hundreds of stalls selling a wide range of goods. The most reliable estimates put the number of large markets in the country at somewhere between 380 and 730. There are many more smaller ones. According to the most reliable estimates, around three-quarters of the North Korean population depends partly or solely on private market activity in order to survive.

CARLOS BARRIA / REUTERS

Workers stand on the deck of the Mangyongbyong cruise ship, operated by the North Korean state tourism agency, September 2011.

In addition to these so-called gray markets, which have made it easier to distribute banned technologies and media, the more conventional black market has also aided the influx of outside information. North Korea currently derives much of its GDP from drug production and trafficking, currency counterfeiting, and money laundering. The illicit networks that support such activities have also created distribution opportunities for foreign media. Today, a motley crew of foreign nongovernmental organizations, defectors, smugglers, middlemen, businessmen, and bribable North Korean soldiers and officials have cobbled together a surprisingly robust network that links ordinary citizens to the outside world through contraband cell phones, laptops, tablet computers, and data drives.

These digital goods have come to play an important (although often invisible) role in North Korean society. Thanks to smuggled media, more North Koreans than ever before now fully perceive the gap between the rosy picture that the regime paints of their country and its leaders and the far grimmer reality. Just as important, many have come to understand that the outside world hardly resembles the wasteland of deprivation, immorality, and criminality that official propaganda depicts.

This burgeoning awareness poses little short-term danger for the regime of Kim Jong Un, which remains highly capable of repressing its people. But in a totalitarian society where the authorities' legitimacy and power depend to a large extent on their ability to delude the population, a growing digital underground might represent a long-term existential threat.

With its expanding nuclear arsenal and penchant for provocation, North Korea is sure to remain a potential source of regional (and even global) instability for a long time to come no matter what outsiders do. But governments, organizations, and individuals seeking ways to make North Korea a less repressive place and a less dangerous international actor should take heed of the power of information to change the country from the inside.

COMBATING JUCHE

On June 11, 2012, a flash flood hit Sinhung County, in the North Korean province of South Hamgyong. A 14-year-old schoolgirl named Han Hyon Gyong desperately tried to keep her family's portraits of the country's founder, Kim Il Sung, and his son and successor, Kim Jong Il, above the floodwaters. She drowned trying to save the sacred images.

For her efforts, the government posthumously granted her the Kim Jong Il Youth Prize. Her parents, teacher, and Youth League leaders also received awards, for helping foster her patriotism. Han's school was renamed after her, and the country's official newspaper, Rodong Sinmun, praised the system that "nurtures such children."

Such extreme devotion to the regime reflects the power of juche, North Korean's official ideology, which emphasizes the country's self-sufficiency and venerates the rulers of the Kim dynasty as quasi deities whose judgment and wisdom may never be questioned. In 1974, Kim Jong Il sought to systematize juche by issuing a list called "Ten Principles for the Establishment of the One-Ideology System"; most of the principles involved acknowledging the absolute authority of the supreme leader and pledging total obedience to the state. Kim demanded that all North Korean citizens memorize the principles and adhere to them in their daily lives, an order enforced through weekly "self-criticism" sessions and peer surveillance. This practice continues today. During weekly meetings in classrooms, offices, and factories, citizens recite the ten principles and are called on to criticize themselves and one another for failing to live in perfect accordance with juche. North Koreans begin participating in these sessions around the time they enter first grade.

Having inculcated juche into its citizens from a very young age, the state does everything it can to ensure that as they grow older, they are exposed to as little contradictory information as possible. One of the most serious crimes that a North Korean can commit is to consume banned media. According to Freedom House, "listening to unauthorized foreign broadcasts and possessing dissident publications are considered 'crimes against the state'" in North Korea and "carry serious punishments, including hard labor, prison sentences, and the death penalty." On a single day in 2013, according to JoongAng Ilbo, a major South Korean newspaper, the government executed 80 people in seven cities for violating such laws.

Jason Lee / Reuters

Portraits of former North Korean leaders Kim Il Sung and Kim Jong Il hang in Pyongyang, July 2013.

Every North Korean household has a statesanctioned radio that broadcasts official propaganda throughout the day. The volume of these radios can be adjusted, but they cannot be turned off entirely. The tuners are disabled. All news reports and broadcasts go through several rounds of internal censorship before they appear. Kim Jong Il's book Guidance for Journalists instructs reporters and editors "to carry articles in which they unfailingly hold the president in high esteem, adore him and praise him as the great revolutionary leader"—instructions that they faithfully follow.

With the exception of a few hundred or perhaps a few thousand elites, North Koreans have no Internet access. Schools, public libraries, and offices are served by a hived-off intranet system known as Kwangmyong. Trusted officials are tasked with scouring the Internet for material that they deem safe enough to add to the closed network, such as select scientific articles and health-related information.

All households have to register their electronic media equipment with local authorities. Occasionally, inspectors go door-to-door to see what's inside people's media players. If they find illegal content, they make arrests and seize the contraband, which they send to their superiors in Pyongyang. Prior to the spread of USB drives, forbidden movies and TV shows were often smuggled into the country on DVDs. To prevent people from quickly ejecting and hiding banned DVDs when a raid began, inspectors would shut off the electricity for an entire apartment building before entering it, trapping discs inside players. The inspectors would then confiscate all the DVD players, turn the electricity back on, plug them in, and press the eject buttons to find out what the residents had been watching.

Such efforts highlight just how nervous digital technologies make the regime. But they are a double-edged sword that also gives the government a tool to better surveil its people and inundate them with still more propaganda. Take mobile phones. North Korea, with an estimated population of around 25 million, now has around three million cell phone users. Almost all of them are limited to the state-run Koryolink provider and network and can make only domestic calls, which are subject to frequent monitoring. But some people now have illegal phones that have been smuggled into North Korea for use near the border, where they can connect to Chinese cellular networks. The security services use detectors that can track down illicit calls that last longer than five minutes. So to avoid detection, one must make a brief call, relocate, then call again to continue the conversation.

Families huddle close together to watch illicit movies and TV shows.

Cell phones can carry content that authorities don't want people to see, but they are also easier to track than other conduits of illegal information. Data transfers are monitored tightly and can alert authorities to anyone who might be accessing banned material. Police officers often stop mobile phone users on the street to inspect their devices for sensitive content; the officers sometimes seize phones and mete out punishments on the spot. Koryolink has incrementally added features such as cameras to its devices and has slowly rolled out services such as text messaging and video calling. Users are now able to access approved intranet sites, including that of Rodong Sinmun; they can also receive text messages from the ruling Korean Workers' Party.

More problematic from the regime's perspective are portable media players, since they are harder to track than cell phones. Many North Koreans can now purchase black-market Chinese-made MP4 devices that play videos stored on smuggled memory cards. MP4 players are small, and their rechargeable batteries last for about two hours at a time, allowing people to watch movies without needing to plug in—a crucial feature, since most North Korean households lack uninterrupted access to electricity.

North Koreans have also embraced the Notetel, a portable device that can access media like a computer does—via USB drives, memory cards, and DVDs—but also functions like a television and a radio. These Chinese-made devices began appearing on the black market around 2005 and cost the equivalent of $30–$50, depending on the model. The regime cracked down on them at first but then legalized the popular devices in 2014 after requiring that all Notetels be registered with local authorities. Since last summer, however, defector-led news organizations have reported that the regime has reversed course and is back to prohibiting the possession of these devices.

Inspectors sometimes burst into a home and check to see if any media players are warm from use. To prepare for that event, many Notetel users keep a legal North Korean DVD in their device at all times so that during a raid they can pull out the USB drive holding the illegal media that they've actually been watching, conceal it, and pretend they'd been using the legal DVD all along. The power, and danger, of Notetels is that they overcome "the twin barriers to foreign media consumption—surveillance and power outages," Sokeel Park of Liberty in North Korea, a nongovernmental organization based in California, told Reuters in March 2015. "If you were to design the perfect device for North Koreans, it would be this."

North Korea viewed from the Chinese side of the Yalu River, September 2016.

Of course, North Koreans don't just have to worry about the authorities: their neighbors could also report them for suspicious activity. So North Koreans have developed various security protocols for watching banned media. Doors are locked, windows are closed, curtains are drawn. Some people hide under blankets with their devices. Families huddle close together to watch illicit movies and TV shows, sometimes sharing earbud headphones—which, if held in just the right position, produce enough sound for a few people to hear but not enough to leak through the walls.

THE JANGMADANG GENERATION

The North Koreans most affected by the influx of digital technology are young people. They enjoy historically unprecedented access to foreign information—which, according to many defectors, is undermining the grip that juche has traditionally held on young North Korean minds.

Every young defector I have met had watched foreign films and shows, had read foreign books, and knew a decent amount about the world outside North Korea before escaping the country. Defectors say that they are not unrepresentative in this respect and that many young North Koreans with no interest in leaving their country nevertheless take the risk of obtaining and consuming foreign media. As Min Jun, a recent defector in his early 20s, told me, "In our generation, young people get together quietly in each other's homes, put on South Korean K-pop, and have a little dance party. We have no idea if we're doing it right, but we dance with the music on low."

On its own, such exposure to foreign culture probably wouldn't mean much. But a number of other factors also set young North Koreans apart from older generations and increase the salience of their access to outside media and digital technology. First, those younger than 35—about a quarter of the population—are known as the jangmadang generation because they came of age buying food and other goods at those small, semilegal markets. They have rarely, if ever, stood in lines to collect state-allotted rations, as their parents and grandparents did for decades. As a result, they are more capitalistic, more individualistic, and more likely to take risks. Black and gray markets offer young people a very particular kind of education, and participating in them leads to a certain kind of savvy: in a society obsessed with rules, young North Koreans have learned how to skirt some of them.

Second, younger North Koreans see themselves as more self-reliant than their parents, because they don't feel as though they've received much of value from their government. Partly for this reason, some North Korea experts see this younger generation as far less loyal to the state and its leadership. "These people are, compared to their parents, much more pragmatic; they are cynical, individualistic; they do not believe in the official ideology," noted Andrei Lankov, a leading expert on North Korea, in a 2015 interview with the South Korean program Arirang News. "They mistrust the government. They are less fearful of the government compared to their parents."

Although young North Koreans continue to obey the laws and publicly respect the regime, young defectors frequently claim that behind closed doors, their friends back home frequently mock the country's leadership.

SMUGGLING IN THE TRUTH

As North Koreans have developed a more accurate perception of their country and the world, many have begun to feel a profound sense of betrayal. That feeling, in turn, has fed a sense of distrust—one that could prove corrosive in a totalitarian state built around a fanatical cult of personality.

For any real political change to take place, however, such distrust would need to spur collective action—a big challenge, given the government's ruthless prohibition of any group activity not expressly sanctioned by the authorities. The regime forbids the formation of unofficial student groups and sports teams. Without express permission, North Koreans are not allowed to host a social gathering late at night or stay overnight away from their hometown in another person's home. The regime has also made it extremely difficult for North Koreans to trust one another by developing a massive network of neighborhood-level informants and offering rewards for exposing anyone who criticizes the government. Finally, the authorities have vastly improved their ability to monitor digital communications, making it extraordinarily difficult to send sensitive messages, much less organize.

Despite these challenges, anyone with an interest in reducing the threat that the Kim regime poses to its own people and to the rest of the world should find ways to support the distribution of foreign information and media in North Korea. Traditional diplomacy and sanctions have failed to push Kim toward political and economic reform and away from saber rattling and defiance. For decades, some of the world's most persistent and skilled negotiators have sought to engage, entice, and coerce him, his father, and his grandfather. But nothing has worked. If major powers have undertaken covert actions to encourage a coup, those too have failed. Meanwhile, Pyongyang's nuclear weapons now deter any overt attempts at regime change and the use of major military force.

If North Korea is going to change, it will have to change from within. Boosting the flow of outside information and cultural products may well be the single most sustainable and cost-effective way to encourage that. Governments, philanthropic groups, and individual donors interested in the future of North Korea should consider funding nongovernmental organizations in South Korea, the United States, and elsewhere that work to get digital technology and foreign media into the country. Especially important are efforts to get outside information into the hands of North Korean military officers, intellectuals, and political elites. Also of great value are projects by nongovernmental organizations to train North Korean defectors—who know the target audience quite well—to assist in collecting media products and getting them across the border.

Critics of such efforts claim that North Korean authorities will have little trouble cracking down if they come to believe that a line has been crossed and that too much illicit information is reaching the public. But this position is too dismissive of the intense thirst for foreign media that North Koreans have displayed. It is difficult to envision how the regime could sustainably ramp up its repression: if its harsh measures have not deterred people from seeking out and consuming banned media, it's hard to imagine what would. North Koreans have tasted forbidden fruit and have made it clear that they want more, risking severe punishment just to steal a glimpse of the outside world while hiding under the covers in a dark, locked room, hoping no one will find out.

JIEUN BAEK is the author of *North Korea's Hidden Revolution: How the Information Underground Is Transforming a Closed Society* (Yale University Press, 2016), from which this essay is adapted. From 2014 to 2016, she was a Fellow at the Belfer Center for Science and International Affairs at Harvard University. Follow her on Twitter @JieunBaek1.

Advice for Young Muslims

How to Survive in an Age of Extremism and Islamophobia

Omar Saif Ghobash

Keeping the faith: a schoolgirl in Sanaa, Yemen, July 2015.

Saif, the elder of my two sons, was born in December 2000. In the summer of 2001, my wife and I brought him with us on a visit to New York City. I remember carrying him around town in a sling on my chest. A few days after we got back home to Dubai, we watched the terrible events of 9/11 unfold on CNN. As it became clear that the attacks had been carried out by jihadist terrorists, I came to feel a new sense of responsibility toward my son, beyond the already intense demands of parenthood. I wanted to open up areas of thought, language, and imagination in order to show him—and to show myself and all my fellow Muslims—that the world offers so much more than the twisted fantasies of extremists. I've tried to do this for the past 15 years. The urgency of the task has seemed only to grow, as the world has become ever more enmeshed in a cycle of jihadist violence and Islamophobia.

Today, I am the ambassador of the United Arab Emirates to Russia, and I try to bring to my work an attitude of openness to ideas and possibilities. In that spirit, I have written a series of letters to Saif, with the intention of opening his eyes to some of the questions he is likely to face as he grows up, and to a range of possible answers. I want my sons and their generation of Muslims to understand how to be faithful to Islam and its deepest values while charting a course through a complex world. I want them to discover through observation and thought that there need be no conflict between Islam and the rest of the world. I want them to understand that even in matters of religion, there are many choices that we must make. I want my sons' generation of Muslims to realize that they have the right—and the obligation—to think about and to decide what is right and what is wrong, what is Islamic and what is peripheral to the faith.

RESPONSIBILITY

Dear Saif,

How should you and I take responsibility for our lives as Muslims? Surely, the most important thing is to be a good person. And if we are good people, then what connection could there be between us and those who commit acts of terrorism, claiming to act in the name of Islam?

Many Muslims protest against and publicly condemn such crimes. Others say that the violent extremists who belong to groups such as the Islamic State (or ISIS) are not true Muslims. "Those people have nothing to do with Islam," is their refrain. To my ears, this statement does not sound right.

It seems like an easy way of not thinking through some difficult questions.

Although I loathe what the terrorists do, I realize that according to the minimal entry requirements for Islam, they are Muslims. Islam demands only that a believer affirm that there is no God but Allah and that Muhammad is his messenger. Violent jihadists certainly believe this. That is why major religious institutions in the Islamic world have rightly refused to label them as non-Muslims, even while condemning their actions. It is too easy to say that jihadist extremists have nothing to do with us. Even if their readings of Islamic Scripture seem warped and out of date, they have gained traction. What worries me is that as the extremists' ideas have spread, the circle of Muslims clinging to other conceptions of Islam has begun to shrink. And as it has shrunk, it has become quieter and quieter, until only the extremists seem to speak and act in the name of Islam.

We need to speak out, but it is not enough to declare in public that Islam is not violent or radical or angry, that Islam is a religion of peace. We need to take responsibility for the Islam of peace. We need to demonstrate how it is expressed in our lives and the lives of those in our community.

People listen to music during Eid Mela in Birmingham, England, August 2013.

I am not saying that Muslims such as you and I should accept blame for what terrorists do. I am saying that we can take responsibility by demanding a different understanding of Islam. We can make clear, to Muslims and non-Muslims, that another reading of Islam is possible and necessary. And we need to act in ways that make clear how we understand Islam and its operation in our lives. I believe we owe that to all the innocent people, both Muslim and non-Muslim, who have suffered at the hands of our coreligionists in their misguided extremism.

Taking that sort of responsibility is hard, especially when many people outside the Muslim world have become committed Islamophobes, fearing and even hating people like you and me, sometimes with the encouragement of political leaders. When you feel unjustly singled out and attacked, it is not easy to look at your beliefs and think them through, especially in a public way. Words and ideas are slippery and can easily slide out of your control. You may be certain of your beliefs about something today, only to wake up with doubts tomorrow. To admit this in today's environment is risky; many Muslims are leery of acknowledging any qualms about their own beliefs. But trust me: it is entirely normal to wonder whether you really got something right.

Some of the greatest scholars of Islam went through periods of confusion and doubt. Consider the philosopher and theologian Abu Hamid al-Ghazali, who was born in Persia in the eleventh century and has been hugely influential in Islamic thought. His works are treasured today, but during his own lifetime, he was so doubtful about many things that he withdrew from society for a decade. He seemed to have experienced a spiritual crisis. Although we don't know much about what troubled him, it's clear that he was unsure and even fearful. But the outcome of his period of doubt and self-imposed isolation was positive: Ghazali, who until then had been esteemed as a scholar of orthodox Islam, brought Sufism, a spiritual strain of Islam, into the mainstream. He opened up Islamic religious experience to spiritualism and poetry, which at that time many considered foreign to the faith.

Today, some of our fellow Muslims demand that we accept only ideas that are Muslim in origin—namely, ideas that appear in the Koran, the early dictionaries of the Arabic language, the sayings of the Prophet, and the biographies of the Prophet and his Companions. Meanwhile, we must reject foreign ideas such as democracy, they maintain. Confronted with more liberal views, which present discussion, debate, and consensus building as ancient Islamic traditions, they contend that democracy is a sin against Allah's power, against his will, and against his sovereignty. Some extremists are even willing to kill in defense of that position.

But do such people even know what democracy is? I don't think so. In fact, from reading many of their statements, it is clear that they have little understanding of how people can come together to make communal decisions. The government that I represent is a monarchy, but I feel no need to condemn proponents of democratic reform as heretics. I might not always agree with them, but their ideas are not necessarily un-Islamic.

As extremist ideas have spread, the circle of Muslims clinging to other conceptions of Islam has begun to shrink.

Another "foreign" practice that causes a great deal of concern to Muslims is the mixing of the sexes. Some Muslim-majority countries mandate the separation of the sexes in schools, universities, and the workplace. (In our own country, most public primary and secondary schools are single sex, as are some universities.) Authorities in these countries present such rules as being "truly Islamic" and argue that they solve the problem of illicit relationships outside of marriage. Perhaps that's true. But research and study of such issues—which is often forbidden—might show that no such effect exists.

And even if rigorous sex separation has some benefits, what are the costs? Could it be that it leads to psychological confusion and turmoil for men and women alike? Could it lead to an inability to understand members of the opposite sex when one is finally allowed to interact with them? Governments in much of the Muslim world have no satisfactory answers to those questions, because they often don't bother to ask them.

MEN AND WOMEN

Dear Saif,

You have been brought up in a household where women—including your mother—are strong, educated, focused, and hard-working. If someone suggested to you that men are somehow more valuable or more talented than women, you would scratch your head. But when I was your age, the sermons that I heard at mosque taught that women were inherently inferior. Men were strong, intelligent, and emotionally stable—natural breadwinners. Women were appendages: objects to be cared for but not to be taken seriously.

That view of women persists in parts of the Muslim world—and, in fairness, in many other places, as well. It is certainly not the only possible view of women afforded by Islam, but it is a powerful belief, and one that enjoys a great deal of political, legal, and financial support.

I am proud that your mother and your aunts are all educated and work in professions that they chose. Doing so has hardly stopped any of them from raising families and taking care of their husbands—the roles demanded by conservative readings of Islamic texts. The women in your life defy the strict traditionalist view, which presents women as fundamentally passive creatures whom men must protect from the ravages of the world. That belief is sometimes self-fulfilling: in many Muslims communities, men insist that women are unable to face the big, wild world, all the while depriving women of the basic rights and skills they would need in order to do so.

Other traditionalists base their position on women on a different argument, one that is rarely discussed openly, especially in front of non-Muslims, because it is a bit of a taboo. It boils down to this: if women were mobile, and independent, and working with men who were not family members, then they might develop illicit romantic or even sexual relationships. Of course, that is a possibility. But such relationships also develop when a woman lives in a home where she is given little love and self-respect. And all too often, women are punished for such relationships, whereas the men involved escape censure—an unacceptable inconsistency.

This traditionalist position is based, ultimately, on a desire to control women. But women do not need to be controlled; they need to be trusted and respected. We trust and respect our sisters, our mothers, our daughters, and our aunts; we must provide the same trust and respect to other women. If we did, perhaps we would not witness so many cases of sexual harassment and exploitation in the Muslim world.

Saif, I want you to see that there is nothing written in stone that places Muslim women below Muslim men. Treating women as inferior is not a religious duty; it is simply a practice of patriarchal societies. Within the Islamic tradition, there are many models of how Muslim women can live and be true to their faith. There are Muslim women, for example, who have looked into the origins of the hijab (the traditional veil that covers the head and hair) and have concluded that there is no hard-and-fast rule requiring them to wear it—let alone a rule requiring them to wear a burqa or a niqab, which both cover far more. Many men have come to the same conclusion. Islam calls on women to be modest in their appearance, but veiling is actually a pre-Islamic tradition.

The limits placed on women in conservative Muslim societies, such as mandatory veiling, or rules limiting their mobility, or restrictions on work and education, have their roots not in Islamic doctrine but rather in men's fear that they will not be able to control women—and their fear that women, if left uncontrolled, will overtake men by being more disciplined, more focused, more hard-working.

STEPHANIE KEITH / REUTERS

At the annual Muslim Day Parade in New York, September 2016.

ISLAM AND THE STATE

Dear Saif,

You will inevitably come across Muslims who shake their heads at the state of affairs in the Islamic world and mutter, "If only people were proper Muslims, then none of this would be happening." I have heard this lament so many times. People say it when criticizing official corruption in Muslim countries and when pointing out the alleged spread of immorality. Others say it when promoting various forms of

Islamic rule. The most famous iteration of this expression is the slogan "Islam Is the Solution," which has been used by the Muslim Brotherhood and many other Islamist groups.

It's a brilliant slogan. Lots of people believe in it. (When I was younger, I believed in it wholeheartedly.) The slogan is a shorthand for the argument that all the most glorious achievements in Islamic history—the conquests, the empires, the knowledge production, the wealth—occurred under some system of religious rule. Therefore, if we want to revive this past glory in the modern era, we must reimpose such a system. This argument holds that if a little Islam is good, then more Islam must be even better. And if more Islam is better, then complete Islam must be best.

The most influential proponent of that position today is ISIS, with its unbridled enthusiasm for an all-encompassing religious state, or caliphate. It can be difficult to argue against that position without seeming to dispute the nature of Islam's origins: the Prophet Muhammad was, after all, not only a religious leader but a political one, too. And the Islamist argument rests on the inexorable logic of extreme faith: if we declare that we are acting in Allah's name, and if we impose the laws of Islam, and if we ensure the correct mental state of the Muslim population living in a chosen territory, then Allah will intervene to solve all our problems. The genius of this proposition—whether it is articulated by the fanatical jihadists of ISIS or the more subtle theocrats of the Muslim Brotherhood—is that any difficulties or failures can be attributed to the people's lack of faith and piety. Leaders need not fault themselves or their policies; citizens need not question their values or customs.

But piety will take us only so far, and relying entirely on Allah to provide for us, to solve our problems, to feed and educate and clothe our children, is to take Allah for granted. The only way we can improve the lot of the Muslim world is by doing what people elsewhere have done, and what Muslims in earlier eras did, in order to succeed: educate ourselves and work hard and engage with life's difficult questions rather than retreat into religious obscurantism.

THE MUSLIM INDIVIDUAL

Dear Saif,

At school, at the mosque, and in the news, you have probably heard a lot about the Arab nation, the Arab street, the rightly guided people, and the Islamic ummah. But have you ever heard people talk about the Muslim individual or about Muslim individualism? Probably not—and that is a problem.

The Prophet spoke about the ummah, or the Muslim community. In the seventh century, that made sense. Out of nothing, Muhammad had built a large group of followers; at some stage, it became big enough to be referred to as a distinct entity. But the concept of the ummah has allowed self-appointed religious authorities to speak in the name of all Muslims without ever asking the rest of us what we think. The idea of an ummah also makes it easier for extremists to depict Islam—and all of the world's Muslims—as standing in opposition to the West, or to capitalism, or to any number of other things. In that conception of the Muslim world, the individual's voice comes second to the group's voice.

We have been trained over the years to put community ahead of individuality. That is why it sounds odd to even speak of "the Muslim individual." The phrase itself sounds almost unnatural to me, as though it refers to a category that doesn't exist—at least in the worldview that Muslims have long been encouraged to embrace.

There is no need to return to a glorious past in order to build a glorious future.

I don't want that to be the case for you and your generation. Dialogue and public debate about what it means to be an individual in the Muslim world would allow us to think more clearly about personal responsibility, ethical choices, and the respect and dignity that attaches to people rather than to families, tribes, or sects. It might lead us to stop insisting solely on our responsibilities to the ummah and start considering our responsibilities to ourselves and to others, whom we might come to see not as members of groups allegedly opposed to Islam but rather as individuals. Instead of asking one another about family names and bloodlines and sects, we might decide to respect one another as individuals regardless of our backgrounds. We might begin to more deeply acknowledge the outrageous number of people killed in the Muslim world in civil wars and in terrorist attacks carried out not by outsiders but by other Muslims. We might memorialize these people not as a group but as individuals with names and faces and life stories—not to deify the dead but rather to recognize our responsibility to preserve their honor and dignity, and the honor and dignity of those who survive them.

In this way, the idea of the Muslim individual might help us improve how we discuss politics, economics, and security. If you and other members of your generation start looking at yourselves as individuals first and foremost, perhaps you will build better societies. You might take hold of your fates and take hold of your lives in the here and now, recognizing that there is no need to return to a glorious past in order to build a glorious future. Our personal, individual interests might not align with those of the patriarch, the family, the tribe, the community, or the state. But the embrace of each Muslim's individuality will lead to a rebalancing in the Islamic world in favor of more compassion, more understanding, and more empathy. If you accept the individual diversity of your fellow Muslims, you are more likely to do the same for those of other faiths, as well.

Muslims can and should live in harmony with the diversity of humanity that exists outside of our faith. But we will struggle to do so until we truly embrace ourselves as individuals.

OMAR SAIF GHOBASH is Ambassador of the United Arab Emirates to Russia. He is the author of *Letters to a Young Muslim* (Picador, 2017), from which this essay is adapted.

The Jacksonian Revolt

American Populism and the Liberal Order

Walter Russell Mead

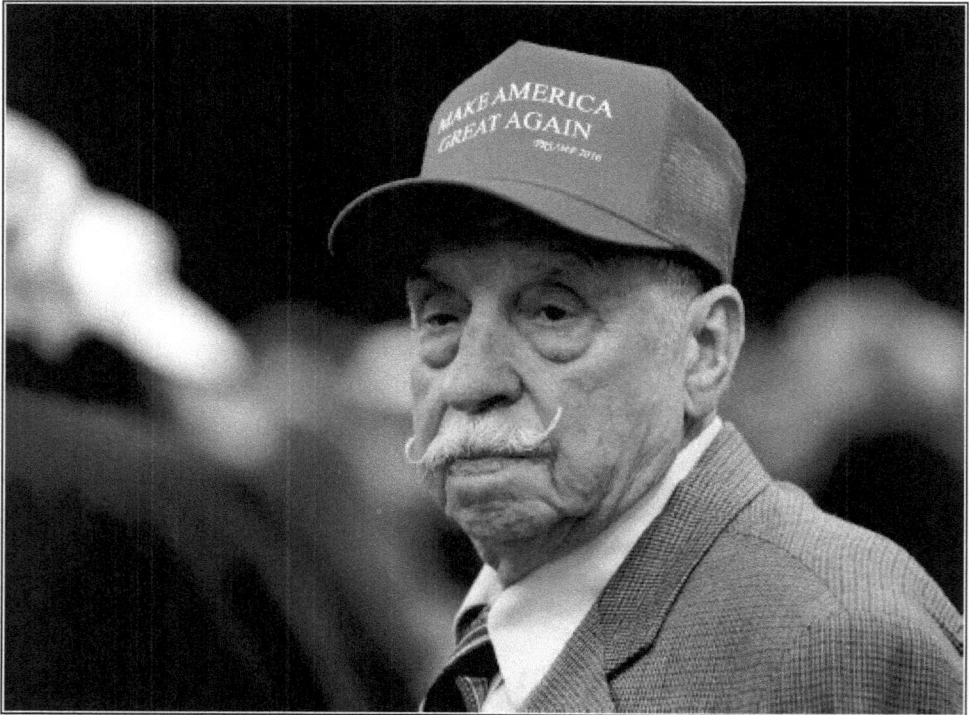

My country, 'tis of me: at a Trump rally in Louisville, Kentucky, March 2016

For the first time in 70 years, the American people have elected a president who disparages the policies, ideas, and institutions at the heart of postwar U.S. foreign policy. No one knows how the foreign policy of the Trump administration will take shape, or how the new president's priorities and preferences will shift as he encounters the torrent of events and crises ahead. But not since Franklin Roosevelt's administration has U.S. foreign policy witnessed debates this fundamental.

Since World War II, U.S. grand strategy has been shaped by two major schools of thought, both focused on achieving a stable international system with the United States at the center. Hamiltonians believed that it was in the American interest for the United States to replace the United Kingdom as "the gyroscope of world order," in the words of President Woodrow Wilson's adviser Edward House during World War I, putting the financial and security architecture in place for a reviving global economy after World War II—something that would both contain the Soviet Union and advance U.S. interests. When the Soviet Union fell, Hamiltonians responded by doubling down on the creation of a global liberal order, understood primarily in economic terms.

Wilsonians, meanwhile, also believed that the creation of a global liberal order was a vital U.S. interest, but they conceived of it in terms of values rather than economics. Seeing corrupt and authoritarian regimes abroad as a leading cause of conflict and violence, Wilsonians sought peace through the promotion of human rights, democratic governance, and the rule of law. In the later stages of the Cold War, one branch of this camp, liberal institutionalists, focused on the promotion of international institutions and ever-closer global integration, while another branch, neoconservatives, believed that a liberal agenda could best be advanced through Washington's unilateral efforts (or in voluntary conjunction with like-minded partners).

The disputes between and among these factions were intense and consequential, but they took place within a common commitment to a common project of global order. As that project came under increasing strain in recent decades, however, the unquestioned grip of the globalists on U.S. foreign policy thinking began to loosen. More nationalist, less globally minded voices began to be heard, and a public increasingly disenchanted with what it saw as the costly failures the global order-building project began to challenge what the foreign policy establishment was preaching. The Jeffersonian and Jacksonian schools of thought, prominent before World War II but out of favor during the heyday of the liberal order, have come back with a vengeance.

Jeffersonians, including today's so-called realists, argue that reducing the United States' global profile would reduce the costs and risks of foreign policy. They seek to define U.S. interests narrowly and advance them in the safest and most economical ways. Libertarians take this proposition to its limits and find allies among many on the left who oppose interventionism, want to cut military spending, and favor redeploying the government's efforts and resources at home. Both Senator Rand Paul of Kentucky and Senator Ted Cruz of Texas seemed to think that they could surf the rising tide of Jeffersonian thinking during the Republican presidential primary. But Donald Trump sensed something that his political rivals failed to grasp: that the truly surging force in American politics wasn't Jeffersonian minimalism. It was Jacksonian populist nationalism.

Celebrating Trump's victory outside the White House, November 9 2016

IDENTITY POLITICS BITE BACK

The distinctively American populism Trump espouses is rooted in the thought and culture of the country's first populist president, Andrew Jackson. For Jacksonians—who formed the core of Trump's passionately supportive base—the United States is not a political entity created and defined by a set of intellectual propositions rooted in the Enlightenment and oriented toward the fulfillment of a universal mission. Rather, it is the nation-state of the American people, and its chief business lies at home. Jacksonians see American exceptionalism not as a function of the universal appeal of American ideas, or even as a function of a unique American vocation to transform the world, but rather as rooted in the country's singular commitment to the equality and dignity of individual American citizens. The role of the U.S. government, Jacksonians believe, is to fulfill the country's destiny by looking after the physical security and economic well-being of the American people in their national home—and to do that while interfering as little as possible with the individual freedom that makes the country unique.

Jacksonian populism is only intermittently concerned with foreign policy, and indeed it is only intermittently engaged with politics more generally. It took a particular combination of forces and trends to mobilize it this election cycle, and most of those were domestically focused. In seeking to explain the Jacksonian surge, commentators have looked to factors such as wage stagnation, the loss of good jobs for unskilled workers, the hollowing out of civic life, a rise in drug use—conditions many associate with life in blighted inner cities that have spread across much of the country. But this is a partial and incomplete view. Identity and culture have historically played a major role in American politics, and 2016 was no exception. Jacksonian America felt itself to be under siege, with its values under attack and its future under threat. Trump—flawed as many Jacksonians themselves believed him to be—seemed the only candidate willing to help fight for its survival.

Not since Franklin Roosevelt's administration has U.S. foreign policy witnessed debates this fundamental.

For Jacksonian America, certain events galvanize intense interest and political engagement, however brief. One of these is war; when an enemy attacks, Jacksonians spring to the country's defense. The most powerful driver of Jacksonian political engagement in domestic politics, similarly, is the perception that Jacksonians are being attacked by internal enemies, such as an elite cabal or immigrants from different backgrounds. Jacksonians worry about the U.S. government being taken over by malevolent forces bent on transforming the United States' essential character. They are not obsessed with corruption, seeing it as an ineradicable part of politics. But they care deeply about what they see as perversion—when politicians try to use the government to oppress the people rather than protect them. And that is what many Jacksonians came to feel was happening in recent years, with powerful forces in the American elite, including the political establishments of both major parties, in cahoots against them.

Many Jacksonians came to believe that the American establishment was no longer reliably patriotic, with "patriotism" defined as an instinctive loyalty to the well-being and values of Jacksonian America. And they were not wholly wrong, by their lights. Many Americans with cosmopolitan sympathies see their main ethical imperative as working for the betterment of humanity in general. Jacksonians locate their moral community closer to home, in fellow citizens who share a common national bond. If the cosmopolitans see Jacksonians as backward and chauvinistic, Jacksonians return the favor by seeing the cosmopolitan elite as near treasonous—people who think it is morally questionable to put their own country, and its citizens, first.

Jacksonian distrust of elite patriotism has been increased by the country's selective embrace of identity politics in recent decades. The contemporary American scene is filled with civic, political, and academic movements celebrating various ethnic, racial, gender, and religious identities. Elites have gradually welcomed demands for cultural recognition by African Americans, Hispanics, women, the

LGBTQ community, Native Americans, Muslim Americans. Yet the situation is more complex for most Jacksonians, who don't see themselves as fitting neatly into any of those categories.

Whites who organize around their specific European ethnic roots can do so with little pushback; Italian Americans and Irish Americans, for example, have long and storied traditions in the parade of American identity groups. But increasingly, those older ethnic identities have faded, and there are taboos against claiming a generic European American or white identity. Many white Americans thus find themselves in a society that talks constantly about the importance of identity, that values ethnic authenticity, that offers economic benefits and social advantages based on identity—for everybody but them. For Americans of mixed European background or for the millions who think of themselves simply as American, there are few acceptable ways to celebrate or even connect with one's heritage.

Jacksonians see American exceptionalism not as a function of the universal appeal of American ideas, but as rooted in the country's singular commitment to the equality and dignity of individual American citizens.

There are many reasons for this, rooted in a complex process of intellectual reflection over U.S. history, but the reasons don't necessarily make intuitive sense to unemployed former factory workers and their families. The growing resistance among many white voters to what they call "political correctness" and a growing willingness to articulate their own sense of group identity can sometimes reflect racism, but they need not always do so. People constantly told that they are racist for thinking in positive terms about what they see as their identity, however, may decide that racist is what they are, and that they might as well make the best of it. The rise of the so-called alt-right is at least partly rooted in this dynamic.

The emergence of the Black Lives Matter movement and the scattered, sometimes violent expressions of anti-police sentiment displayed in recent years compounded the Jacksonians' sense of cultural alienation, and again, not simply because of race. Jacksonians instinctively support the police, just as they instinctively support the military. Those on the frontlines protecting society sometimes make mistakes, in this view, but mistakes are inevitable in the heat of combat, or in the face of crime. It is unfair and even immoral, many Jacksonians believe, to ask soldiers or police officers to put their lives on the line and face great risks and stress, only to have their choices second-guessed by armchair critics. Protests that many Americans saw as a quest for justice, therefore, often struck Jacksonians as attacks on law enforcement and public order.

Gun control and immigration were two other issues that crystallized the perception among many voters that the political establishments of both parties had grown hostile to core national values. Non-Jacksonians often find it difficult to grasp the depth of the feelings these issues stir up and how proposals for gun control and immigration reform reinforce suspicions about elite control and cosmopolitanism.

The right to bear arms plays a unique and hallowed role in Jacksonian political culture, and many Jacksonians consider the Second Amendment to be the most important in the Constitution. These Americans see the right of revolution, enshrined in the Declaration of Independence, as the last resort of a free people to defend themselves against tyranny—and see that right as unenforceable without the possibility of bearing arms. They regard a family's right to protect itself without reliance on the state, meanwhile, as not just a hypothetical ideal but a potential practical necessity—and something that elites don't care about or even actively oppose. (Jacksonians have become increasingly concerned that Democrats and centrist Republicans will try to disarm them, which is one reason why mass shootings and subsequent calls for gun control spur spikes in gun sales, even as crime more generally has fallen.)

As for immigration, here, too, most non-Jacksonians misread the source and nature of Jacksonian concern. There has been much discussion about the impact of immigration on the wages of low-skilled workers and some talk about xenophobia and Islamophobia. But Jacksonians in 2016 saw immigration as part of a deliberate and conscious attempt to marginalize them in their own country. Hopeful talk among Democrats about an "emerging Democratic majority" based on a secular decline in the percentage of the voting population that is white was heard in Jacksonian America as support for a deliberate transformation of American demographics. When Jacksonians hear elites' strong support for high levels of immigration and their seeming lack of concern about illegal immigration, they do not immediately think of their pocketbooks. They see an elite out to banish them from power—politically, culturally, demographically. The recent spate of dramatic random terrorist attacks, finally, fused the immigration and personal security issues into a single toxic whole.

In short, in November, many Americans voted their lack of confidence—not in a particular party but in the governing classes more generally and their associated global cosmopolitan ideology. Many Trump voters were less concerned with pushing a specific program than with stopping what appeared to be the inexorable movement of their country toward catastrophe.

Trump at a rally in Doral, Florida, October 2015

THE ROAD AHEAD

What all of this means for U.S. foreign policy remains to be seen. Many previous presidents have had to revise their ideas substantially after reaching the Oval Office; Trump may be no exception. Nor is it clear just what the results would be of trying to put his unorthodox policies into practice. (Jacksonians can become disappointed with failure and turn away from even former heroes they once embraced; this happened to President George W. Bush, and it could happen to Trump, too.)

At the moment, Jacksonians are skeptical about the United States' policy of global engagement and liberal order building—but more from a lack of trust in the people shaping foreign policy than from a desire for a specific alternative vision. They oppose recent trade agreements not because they understand the details and consequences of those extremely complex agreements' terms but because they have come to believe that the negotiators of those agreements did not necessarily have the United States' interests at heart. Most Jacksonians are not foreign policy experts and do not ever expect to become experts. For them, leadership is necessarily a matter of trust. If they believe in a leader or a political movement, they are prepared to accept policies that seem counter-intuitive and difficult.

They no longer have such trust in the American establishment, and unless and until it can be restored, they will keep Washington on a short leash. To paraphrase what the neoconservative intellectual Irving Kristol wrote about Senator Joseph McCarthy in 1952, there is one thing that Jacksonians know about Trump—that he is unequivocally on their side. About their country's elites, they feel they know no such thing. And their concerns are not all illegitimate, for the United States' global order-building project is hardly flourishing.

The right to bear arms plays a unique and hallowed role in Jacksonian political culture.

Over the past quarter century, Western policymakers became infatuated with some dangerously oversimplified ideas. They believed capitalism had been tamed and would no longer generate economic, social, or political upheavals. They felt that illiberal ideologies and political emotions had been left in the historical dustbin and were believed only by "bitter" losers—people who "cling to guns or religion or antipathy toward people who aren't like them . . . as a way to explain their frustrations," as Barack Obama famously put it in 2008. Time and the normal processes of history would solve the problem; constructing a liberal world order was simply a matter of working out the details.

Given such views, many recent developments—from the 9/11 attacks and the war on terrorism to the financial crisis to the recent surge of angry nationalist populism on both sides of the Atlantic—came as a rude surprise. It is increasingly clear that globalization and automation have helped break up the socioeconomic model that undergirded postwar prosperity and domestic social peace, and that the next stage of capitalist development will challenge the very foundations of both the global liberal order and many of its national pillars.

In this new world disorder, the power of identity politics can no longer be denied. Western elites believed that in the twenty-first century, cosmopolitanism and globalism would triumph over atavism and tribal loyalties. They failed to understand the deep roots of identity politics in the human psyche and the necessity for those roots to find political expression in both foreign and domestic policy arenas. And they failed to understand that the very forces of economic and social development that cosmopolitanism and globalization fostered would generate turbulence and eventually resistance, as Gemeinschaft (community) fought back against the onrushing Gesellschaft (market society), in the classic terms sociologists favored a century ago.

The challenge for international politics in the days ahead is therefore less to complete the task of liberal world order building along conventional lines than to find a way to stop the liberal order's erosion and reground the global system on a more sustainable basis. International order needs to rest not just on elite consensus and balances of power and policy but also on the free choices of national communities—communities that need to feel protected from the outside world as much as they want to benefit from engaging with it.

WALTER RUSSELL MEAD is James Clarke Chace Professor of Foreign Affairs and Humanities at Bard College and a Distinguished Scholar at the Hudson Institute. Follow him on Twitter @wrmead.

How America Lost Faith in Expertise

And Why That's a Giant Problem

Tom Nichols

A Harvard Medical School professor waits for commencement ceremonies to begin in Cambridge, May 2011.

In 2014, following the Russian invasion of Crimea, The Washington Post published the results of a poll that asked Americans about whether the United States should intervene militarily in Ukraine. Only one in six could identify Ukraine on a map; the median response was off by about 1,800 miles. But this lack of knowledge did not stop people from expressing pointed views. In fact, the respondents favored intervention in direct proportion to their ignorance. Put another way, the people who thought Ukraine was located in Latin America or Australia were the most enthusiastic about using military force there.

The following year, Public Policy Polling asked a broad sample of Democratic and Republican primary voters whether they would support bombing Agrabah. Nearly a third of Republican respondents said they would, versus 13 percent who opposed the idea. Democratic preferences were roughly reversed; 36 percent were opposed, and 19 percent were in favor. Agrabah doesn't exist. It's the fictional country in the 1992 Disney film Aladdin. Liberals crowed that the poll showed Republicans' aggressive tendencies. Conservatives countered that it showed Democrats' reflexive pacifism. Experts in national security couldn't fail to notice that 43 percent of Republicans and 55 percent of Democrats polled had an actual, defined view on bombing a place in a cartoon.

Increasingly, incidents like this are the norm rather than the exception. It's not just that people don't know a lot about science or politics or geography. They don't, but that's an old problem. The bigger concern today is that Americans have reached a point where ignorance—at least regarding what is generally considered established knowledge in public policy—is seen as an actual virtue. To reject the advice of experts is to assert autonomy, a way for Americans to demonstrate their independence from nefarious elites—and insulate their increasingly fragile egos from ever being told they're wrong.

This isn't the same thing as the traditional American distaste for intellectuals and know-it-alls. I'm a professor, and I get it: most people don't like professors. And I'm used to people disagreeing with me on lots of things. Principled, informed arguments are a sign of intellectual health and vitality in a democracy. I'm worried because we no longer have those kinds of arguments, just angry shouting matches.

When I started working in Washington in the 1980s, I quickly learned that random people I met would instruct me in what the government should do about any number of things, particularly my own specialties of arms control and foreign policy. At first I was surprised, but I came to realize that this was understandable and even to some extent desirable. We live in a democracy, and many people have strong opinions about public life. Over time, I found that other policy specialists had similar experiences, with laypeople subjecting them to lengthy disquisitions on taxes, budgets, immigration, the environment, and many other subjects. If you work on public policy, such interactions go with the job, and at their best, they help keep you intellectually honest.

In later years, however, I started hearing the same stories from doctors and lawyers and teachers and many other professionals. These were stories not about patients or clients or students raising informed questions but about them telling the professionals why their professional advice was actually misguided or even wrong. The idea that the expert was giving considered, experienced advice worth taking seriously was simply dismissed.

I fear we are moving beyond a natural skepticism regarding expert claims to the death of the ideal of expertise itself: a Google-fueled, Wikipedia-based, blog-sodden collapse of any division between professionals and laypeople, teachers and students, knowers and wonderers—in other words, between those with achievement in an area and those with none. By the death of expertise, I do not mean the death of actual expert abilities, the knowledge of specific things that sets some people apart from others in various areas. There will always be doctors and lawyers and engineers and other specialists. And most sane people go straight to them if they break a bone or get arrested or need to build a bridge. But that represents a kind of reliance on experts as technicians, the use of established knowledge as an off-the-shelf convenience as desired. "Stitch this cut in my leg, but don't lecture me about my diet." (More than two-thirds of Americans are overweight.) "Help me beat this tax problem, but don't remind me that I should have a will." (Roughly half of Americans with children haven't written one.) "Keep my country safe, but don't confuse me with details about national security tradeoffs." (Most U.S. citizens have no clue what the government spends on the military or what its policies are on most security matters.)

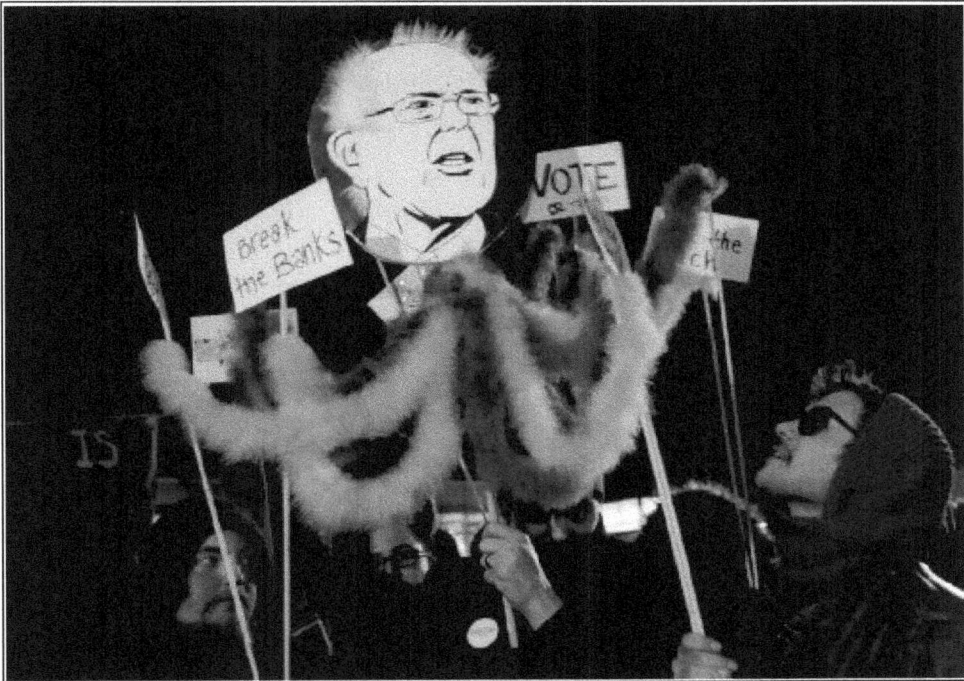

Supporters of Bernie Sanders, then a candidate for the Democratic presidential nomination, outside a rally in Flint, Michigan, April 2016.

The larger discussions, from what constitutes a nutritious diet to what actions will best further U.S. interests, require conversations between ordinary citizens and experts. But increasingly, citizens don't want to have those conversations.

Rather, they want to weigh in and have their opinions treated with deep respect and their preferences honored not on the strength of their arguments or on the evidence they present but based on their feelings, emotions, and whatever stray information they may have picked up here or there along the way.

This is a very bad thing. A modern society cannot function without a social division of labor. No one is an expert on everything. We prosper because we specialize, developing formal and informal mechanisms and practices that allow us to trust one another in those specializations and gain the collective benefit of our individual expertise. If that trust dissipates, eventually both democracy and expertise will be fatally corrupted, because neither democratic leaders nor their expert advisers want to tangle with an ignorant electorate. At that point, expertise will no longer serve the public interest; it will serve the interest of whatever clique is paying its bills or taking the popular temperature at any given moment. And such an outcome is already perilously near.

A LITTLE LEARNING IS A DANGEROUS THING

Over a half century ago, the historian Richard Hofstadter wrote that "the complexity of modern life has steadily whittled away the functions the ordinary citizen can intelligently and comprehendingly perform for himself."

In the original American populistic dream, the omnicompetence of the common man was fundamental and indispensable. It was believed that he could, without much special preparation, pursue the professions and run the government. Today he knows that he cannot even make his breakfast without using devices, more or less mysterious to him, which expertise has put at his disposal; and when he sits down to breakfast and looks at his morning newspaper, he reads about a whole range of vital and intricate issues and acknowledges, if he is candid with himself, that he has not acquired competence to judge most of them.

Hofstadter argued that this overwhelming complexity produced feelings of helplessness and anger among a citizenry that knew itself to be increasingly at the mercy of more sophisticated elites. "What used to be a jocular and usually benign ridicule of intellect and formal training has turned into a malign resentment of the intellectual in his capacity as expert," he noted. "Once the intellectual was gently ridiculed because he was not needed; now he is fiercely resented because he is needed too much."

In 2015, the law professor Ilya Somin observed that the problem had persisted and even metastasized over time. The "size and complexity of government," he wrote, have made it "more difficult for voters with limited knowledge to monitor and evaluate the government's many activities. The result is a polity in which the people often cannot exercise their sovereignty responsibly and effectively." Despite decades of advances in education, technology, and life opportunities, voters now are no better able to guide public policy than they were in Hofstadter's day, and in many respects, they are even less capable of doing so.

The problem cannot be reduced to politics, class, or geography. Today, campaigns against established knowledge are often led by people who have all the tools they need to know better. For example, the anti-vaccine movement—one of the classic contemporary examples of this phenomenon—has gained its greatest reach among people such as the educated suburbanites in Marin County, outside San Francisco, where at the peak of the craze, in 2012, almost eight percent of parents requested a personal belief exemption from the obligation to vaccinate their children before enrolling them in school. These parents were not medical professionals, but they had just enough education to believe that they could challenge established medical science, and they felt empowered to do so—even at the cost of the health of their own and everybody else's children.

DON'T KNOW MUCH

Experts can be defined loosely as people who have mastered the specialized skills and bodies of knowledge relevant to a particular occupation and who routinely rely on them in their daily work. Put another way, experts are the people who know considerably more about a given subject than the rest of us, and to whom we usually turn for education or advice on that topic. They don't know everything, and they're not always right, but they constitute an authoritative minority whose views on a topic are more likely to be right than those of the public at large.

How do we identify who these experts are? In part, by formal training, education, and professional experience, applied over the course of a career. Teachers, nurses, and plumbers all have to acquire certification of some kind to exercise their skills, as a signal to others that their abilities have been reviewed by their peers and met a basic standard of competence. Credentialism can run amok, and guilds can use it cynically to generate revenue or protect their fiefdoms with unnecessary barriers to entry. But it can also reflect actual learning and professional competence, helping separate real experts from amateurs or charlatans.

Beyond credentials lies talent, an immutable but real quality that creates differences in status even within expert communities. And beyond both lies a mindset, an acceptance of membership in a broader community of specialists devoted to ever-greater understanding of a particular subject. Experts agree to evaluation and correction by other experts. Every professional group and expert community has watchdogs, boards, accreditors, and certification authorities whose job is to police its own members and ensure that they are competent and live up to the standards of their own specialty.

Experts are often wrong, and the good ones among them are the first to admit it—because their own professional disciplines are based not on some ideal of perfect knowledge and competence but on a constant process of identifying errors and correcting them, which ultimately drives intellectual progress. Yet these days, members of the public search for expert errors and revel in finding them—not to improve understanding but rather to give themselves license to disregard all expert advice they don't like.

Part of the problem is that some people think they're experts when in fact they're not. We've all been trapped at a party where one of the least informed people in the room holds court, confidently lecturing the other guests with a cascade of banalities and misinformation. This sort of experience isn't just in your imagination. It's real, and it's called "the Dunning-Kruger effect," after the research psychologists David Dunning and Justin Kruger. The essence of the effect is that the less skilled or competent you are, the more confident you are that you're actually very good at what you do. The psychologists' central finding: "Not only do [such people] reach erroneous conclusions and make unfortunate choices, but their incompetence robs them of the ability to realize it."

We are moving toward a Google-fueled, Wikipedia-based collapse of any division between professionals and laypeople.

To some extent, this is true of everybody, in the same way that few people are willing to accept that they have a lousy sense of humor or a grating personality. As it turns out, most people rate themselves higher than others would regarding a variety of skills. (Think of the writer Garrison Keillor's fictional town of Lake Wobegon, where "all the children are above average.") But it turns out that less competent people overestimate themselves more than others do. As Dunning wrote in 2014,

---

A whole battery of studies . . . have confirmed that people who don't know much about a given set of cognitive, technical, or social skills tend to grossly overestimate their prowess and performance, whether it's grammar, emotional intelligence, logical reasoning, firearm care and safety, debating, or financial knowledge. College students who hand in exams that will earn them Ds and Fs tend to think their efforts will be worthy of far higher grades; low-performing chess players, bridge players, and medical students, and elderly people applying for a renewed driver's license, similarly overestimate their competence by a long shot.

The reason turns out to be the absence of a quality called "metacognition," the ability to step back and see your own cognitive processes in perspective. Good singers know when they've hit a sour note, good directors know when a scene in a play isn't working, and intellectually self-aware people know when they're out of their depth. Their less successful counterparts can't tell—which can lead to a lot of bad music, boring drama, and maddening conversations. Worse, it's very hard to educate or inform people who, when in doubt, just make stuff up. The least competent people turn out to be the ones least likely to realize they are wrong and others are right, the most likely to respond to their own ignorance by trying to fake it, and the least able to learn anything.

SURREALITY-BASED COMMUNITY

The problems for democracy posed by the least competent are serious. But even competent and highly intelligent people encounter problems in trying to comprehend complicated issues of public policy with which they are not professionally conversant. Most prominent of those problems is confirmation bias, the tendency to look for information that corroborates what we already believe. Scientists and researchers grapple with this all the time as a professional hazard, which is why, before presenting or publishing their work, they try to make sure their findings are robust and pass a reality check from qualified colleagues without a personal investment in the outcome of the project. This peer-review process is generally invisible to laypeople, however, because the checking and adjustments take place before the final product is released.

Outside the academy, in contrast, arguments and debates usually have no external review or accountability at all. Facts come and go as people find convenient at the moment, making arguments unfalsifiable and intellectual progress impossible. And unfortunately, because common sense is not enough to understand or judge plausible alternative policy options, the gap between informed specialists and uninformed laypeople often gets filled with crude simplifications or conspiracy theories.

Conspiracy theories are attractive to people who have a hard time making sense of a complicated world and little patience for boring, detailed explanations. They are also a way for people to give context and meaning to events that frighten them. Without a coherent explanation for why terrible things happen to innocent people, they would have to accept such occurrences as nothing more than the random cruelty of either an uncaring universe or an incomprehensible deity.

And just as individuals facing grief and confusion look for meaning where none may exist, so, too, will entire societies gravitate toward outlandish theories when collectively subjected to a terrible national experience. Conspiracy theories and the awed reasoning behind them, as the Canadian writer Jonathan Kay has noted, become especially seductive "in any society that has suffered an epic, collectively felt trauma." This is why they spiked in popularity after World War I, the Russian Revolution, the

Kennedy assassination, the 9/11 attacks, and other major disasters—and are growing now in response to destabilizing contemporary trends, such as the economic and social dislocations of globalization and persistent terrorism.

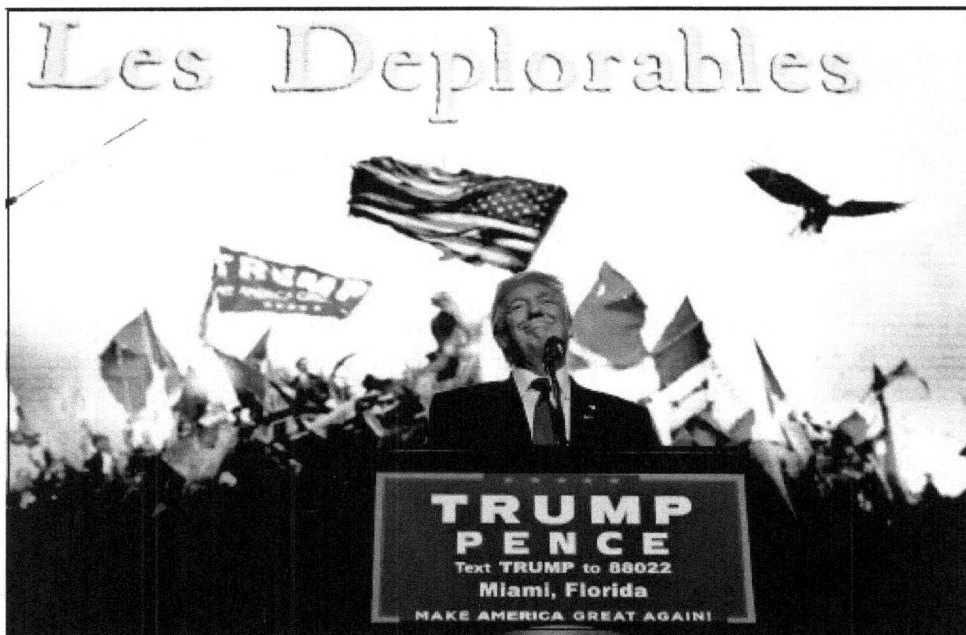

Donald Trump, then a candidate for president of the United States, at a campaign rally in Miami, September 2016.

At their worst, conspiracy theories can produce a moral panic in which innocent people get hurt. But even when they seem trivial, their prevalence undermines the sort of reasoned interpersonal discourse on which liberal democracy depends. Why? Because by definition, conspiracy theories are unfalsifiable: experts who contradict them demonstrate that they, too, are part of the conspiracy.

The addition of politics, finally, makes things even more complicated. Political beliefs among both laypeople and experts are subject to the same confirmation bias that plagues thinking about other issues. But misguided beliefs about politics and other subjective matters are even harder to shake, because political views are deeply rooted in a person's self-image and most cherished beliefs. Put another way, what we believe says something important about how we see ourselves, making disconfirmation of such beliefs a wrenching process that our minds stubbornly resist.

As a result, unable to see their own biases, most people simply drive one another crazy arguing rather than accept answers that contradict what they already think about the subject—and shoot the messenger, to boot. A 2015 study by scholars at Ohio

State University, for example, tested the reactions of liberals and conservatives to certain kinds of news stories and found that both groups tended to discount scientific theories that contradicted their worldviews. Even more disturbing, the study found that when exposed to scientific research that challenged their views, both liberals and conservatives reacted by doubting the science rather than themselves.

WELCOME TO THE IDIOCRACY

Ask an expert about the death of expertise, and you will probably get a rant about the influence of the Internet. People who once had to turn to specialists in any given field now plug search terms into a Web browser and get answers in seconds—so why should they rely on some remote clerisy of snooty eggheads? Information technology, however, is not the primary problem. The digital age has simply accelerated the collapse of communication between experts and laypeople by offering an apparent shortcut to erudition. It has allowed people to mimic intellectual accomplishment by indulging in an illusion of expertise provided by a limitless supply of facts.

But facts are not the same as knowledge or ability—and on the Internet, they're not even always facts. Of all the axiomatic "laws" that describe Internet usage, the most important may be the predigital insight of the science fiction writer Theodore Sturgeon, whose eponymous rule states that "90 percent of everything is crap." More than a billion websites now exist. The good news is that even if Sturgeon's cynicism holds, that yields 100 million pretty good sites—including those of all the reputable publications of the world; the homepages of universities, think tanks, research institutions, and nongovernmental organizations; and vast numbers of other edifying sources of good information.

The countless dumpsters of nonsense parked on the Internet are an expert's nightmare.

The bad news, of course, is that to find any of this, you have to navigate through a blizzard of useless or misleading garbage posted by everyone from well-intentioned grandmothers to propagandists for the Islamic State (or ISIS). Some of the smartest people on earth have a significant presence on the Internet. Some of the stupidest people, however, reside just one click away. The countless dumpsters of nonsense parked on the Internet are an expert's nightmare. Ordinary people who already had to make hard choices about where to get their information when there were a few dozen newspapers, magazines, and television channels now face endless webpages produced by anyone willing to pay for an online presence.

Of course, this is no more and no less than an updated version of the basic paradox of the printing press. As the writer Nicholas Carr pointed out, the arrival of Gutenberg's invention in the fifteenth century set off a "round of teeth gnashing" among early humanists, who worried that "printed books and broadsheets would undermine religious authority, demean the work of scholars and scribes, and spread sedition

and debauchery." The Internet is the printing press at the speed of fiber optics.

The convenience of the Internet is a tremendous boon, but mostly for people already trained in research and who have some idea what they're looking for. It does little good, unfortunately, for a student or an untrained layperson who has never been taught how to judge the provenance of information or the reputability of a writer.

Libraries, or at least their reference and academic sections, once served as a kind of first cut through the noise of the marketplace. The Internet, however, is less a library than a giant repository where anyone can dump anything. In practice, this means that a search for information will rely on algorithms usually developed by for-profit companies using opaque criteria. Actual research is hard and often boring. It requires the ability to find authentic information, sort through it, analyze it, and apply it. But why bother with all that tedious hoop jumping when the screen in front of us presents neat and pretty answers in seconds?

Technological optimists will argue that these objections are just so much old-think, a relic of how things used to be done, and unnecessary now because people can tap directly into the so-called wisdom of crowds. It is true that the aggregated judgments of large groups of ordinary people sometimes produce better results than the judgments of any individual, even a specialist. This is because the aggregation process helps wash out a lot of random misperception, confirmation bias, and the like. Yet not everything is amenable to the vote of a crowd. Understanding how a virus is transmitted from one human being to another is not the same thing as guessing the number of jellybeans in a glass jar. And as the comedian John Oliver has pointed out, you don't need to gather opinions on a fact: "You might as well have a poll asking, 'Which number is bigger, 15 or 5?' or 'Do owls exist?' or 'Are there hats?'"

Moreover, the whole point of the wisdom of crowds is that the members of the crowd supposedly bring to bear various independent opinions on any given topic. In fact, however, the Internet tends to generate communities of the like-minded, groups dedicated to confirming their own preexisting beliefs rather than challenging them. And social media only amplifies this echo chamber, miring millions of Americans in their own political and intellectual biases.

EXPERTISE AND DEMOCRACY

Experts fail often, in various ways. The most innocent and most common are what we might think of as the ordinary failures of science. Individuals, or even entire professions, observe a phenomenon or examine a problem, come up with theories about it or solutions for it, and then test them. Sometimes they're right, and sometimes they're wrong, but most errors are eventually corrected. Intellectual progress includes a lot of blind alleys and wrong turns along the way.

Other forms of expert failure are more worrisome. Experts can go wrong, for example, when they try to stretch their expertise from one area to another. This is less a failure of expertise than a sort of minor fraud—somebody claiming the general mantle of authority even though he or she is not a real expert in the specific area under discussion—and it is frequent and pernicious and can undermine the credibility of an entire field. (I recognize that I myself risk that transgression. But my observations and conclusions are informed not only by my experience of being an expert in my own area but also by the work of scholars who study the role of expertise in society and by discussions I have had with many other experts in a variety of fields.) And finally, there is the rarest but most dangerous category: outright deception and malfeasance, in which experts intentionally falsify their results or rent out their professional authority to the highest bidder.

When they do fail, experts must own their mistakes, air them publicly, and show the steps they are taking to correct them. This happens less than it should in the world of public policy, because the standards for judging policy work tend to be more subjective and politicized than the academic norm. Still, for their own credibility, policy professionals should be more transparent, honest, and self-critical about their far-from-perfect track records. Laypeople, for their part, must educate themselves about the difference between errors and incompetence, corruption, or outright fraud and cut the professionals some slack regarding the former while insisting on punishment for the latter. As the philosopher Bertrand Russell once wrote, the proper attitude of a layperson toward experts should be a combination of skepticism and humility:

The skepticism that I advocate amounts only to this: (1) that when the experts are agreed, the opposite opinion cannot be held to be certain; (2) that when they are not agreed, no opinion can be regarded as certain by a non-expert; and (3) that when they all hold that no sufficient grounds for a positive opinion exist, the ordinary man would do well to suspend his judgment.

As Russell noted, "These propositions may seem mild, yet, if accepted, they would absolutely revolutionize human life"—because the results would challenge so much of what so many people feel most strongly.

Government and expertise rely on each other, especially in a democracy. The technological and economic progress that ensures the well-being of a population requires a division of labor, which in turn leads to the creation of professions. Professionalism encourages experts to do their best to serve their clients, respect their own knowledge boundaries, and demand that their boundaries be respected by others, as part of an overall service to the ultimate client: society itself.

A statue of Theodore Dwight Woolsey, former president of Yale, on Yale's campus in New Haven, Connecticut, November 2012.

Dictatorships, too, demand this same service of experts, but they extract it by threat and direct its use by command. This is why dictatorships are actually less efficient and less productive than democracies (despite some popular stereotypes to the contrary). In a democracy, the expert's service to the public is part of the social contract. Citizens delegate the power of decision on myriad issues to elected representatives and their expert advisers, while experts, for their part, ask that their efforts be received in good faith by a public that has informed itself enough—a key requirement—to make reasoned judgments.

This relationship between experts and citizens rests on a foundation of mutual respect and trust. When that foundation erodes, experts and laypeople become warring factions and democracy itself can become a casualty, decaying into mob rule or elitist technocracy. Living in a world awash in gadgets and once unimaginable conveniences and entertainments, Americans (and many other Westerners) have become almost childlike in their refusal to learn enough to govern themselves or to guide the policies that affect their lives. This is a collapse of functional citizenship, and it enables a cascade of other baleful consequences.

In the absence of informed citizens, for example, more knowledgeable administrative and intellectual elites do in fact take over the daily direction of the state and society. The Austrian economist F. A. Hayek wrote in 1960, "The greatest danger to liberty today comes from the men who are most needed and most powerful in modern government, namely, the efficient expert administrators exclusively concerned with what they regard as the public good."

There is a great deal of truth in this. Unelected bureaucrats and policy specialists in many spheres exert tremendous influence on the daily lives of Americans. Today, however, this situation exists by default rather than design. And populism actually reinforces this elitism, because the celebration of ignorance cannot launch communications satellites, negotiate the rights of U.S. citizens overseas, or provide effective medications. Faced with a public that has no idea how most things work, experts disengage, choosing to speak mostly to one another.

Like anti-vaccine parents, ignorant voters end up punishing society at large for their own mistakes.

Meanwhile, Americans have developed increasingly unrealistic expectations of what their political and economic systems can provide, and this sense of entitlement fuels continual disappointment and anger. When people are told that ending poverty or preventing terrorism or stimulating economic growth is a lot harder than it looks, they roll their eyes. Unable to comprehend all the complexity around them, they choose instead to comprehend almost none of it and then sullenly blame elites for seizing control of their lives.

"A REPUBLIC, IF YOU CAN KEEP IT"

Experts can only propose; elected leaders dispose. And politicians are very rarely experts on any of the innumerable subjects that come before them for a decision. By definition, nobody can be an expert on China policy and health care and climate change and immigration and taxation, all at the same time—which is why during, say, congressional hearings on a subject, actual experts are usually brought in to advise the elected laypeople charged with making authoritative decisions.

In 1787, Benjamin Franklin was supposedly asked what would emerge from the Constitutional Convention being held in Philadelphia. "A republic," Franklin answered, "if you can keep it." Americans too easily forget that the form of government under which they live was not designed for mass decisions about complicated issues. Neither, of course, was it designed for rule by a tiny group of technocrats or experts. Rather, it was meant to be the vehicle by which an informed electorate could choose other people to represent them, come up to speed on important questions, and make decisions on the public's behalf.

The workings of such a representative democracy, however, are exponentially more difficult when the electorate is not competent to judge the matters at hand. Laypeople complain about the rule of experts and demand greater involvement in complicated national questions, but many of them express their anger and make these demands only after abdicating their own important role in the process: namely, to stay informed and politically literate enough to choose representatives who can act wisely on their behalf. As Somin has written, "When we elect government officials based on ignorance, they rule over not only those who voted for them but all of society. When we exercise power over other people, we have a moral obligation to do so in at least a reasonably informed way." Like anti-vaccine parents, ignorant voters end up punishing society at large for their own mistakes.

Too few citizens today understand democracy to mean a condition of political equality in which all get the franchise and are equal in the eyes of the law. Rather, they think of it as a state of actual equality, in which every opinion is as good as any other, regardless of the logic or evidentiary base behind it. But that is not how a republic is meant to work, and the sooner American society establishes new ground rules for productive engagement between educated elites and the society around them, the better.

Experts need to remember, always, that they are the servants of a democratic society and a republican government. Their citizen masters, however, must equip themselves not just with education but also with the kind of civic virtue that keeps them involved in the running of their own country. Laypeople cannot do without experts, and they must accept this reality without rancor. Experts, likewise, must accept that they get a hearing, not a veto, and that their advice will not always be taken. At this point, the bonds tying the system together are dangerously frayed. Unless some sort of trust and mutual respect can be restored, public discourse will be polluted by unearned respect for unfounded opinions. And in such an environment, anything and everything becomes possible, including the end of democracy and republican government itself.

TOM NICHOLS is Professor of National Security Affairs at the U.S. Naval War College. He is the author of *The Death of Expertise: The Campaign Against Established Knowledge and Why It Matters* (Oxford University Press, 2017), from which this essay is adapted. Follow him on Twitter @RadioFreeTom. The views expressed here are his own.

Asia's Other Revisionist Power

Why U.S. Grand Strategy Unnerves China

Jennifer Lind

You started it: Obama and Xi in Paris, November 2015.

Donald Trump's election as U.S. president threatens to upend the world's most important bilateral relationship. On the campaign trail, Trump promised to label China a currency manipulator and to respond to its "theft of American trade secrets" and "unfair subsidy behavior" by levying a 45 percent tariff on Chinese exports. As president-elect, he reversed four decades of U.S. policy when he spoke by telephone with Taiwanese President Tsai Ing-wen and declared that the United States was not bound by the "one China" policy, the diplomatic understanding that has underpinned Washington's approach to Beijing since 1979.

Trump's actions, however, have only compounded deeper problems in the Sino-American relationship. Recent Chinese policies have fueled concerns that the country seeks to overturn the post–Cold War geopolitical order. President Xi Jinping has begun to modernize China's military, gradually transforming the regional balance of power. He has pursued assertive policies in the East China and South China Seas, appearing to reject both the territorial status quo in East Asia and the role of international law in adjudicating disputes. Many observers now believe that efforts to integrate China into the international system have failed and that East Asia will have to contend with a dangerous, revisionist power.

But China is not the only revisionist power in the U.S.-Chinese relationship. Since the end of World War II, the United States has pursued a strategy aimed at overturning the status quo by spreading liberalism, free markets, and U.S. influence around the world. Just as Chinese revisionism alarms Washington, the United States' posture stokes fear in Beijing and beyond. As Trump begins his presidency, he would do well to understand this fear. The risk of crises, and even war, will grow if Trump introduces instability into areas of the relationship that posed few problems under previous U.S. administrations. But Trump could ease tensions if he pursues a less revisionist strategy than his predecessors.

SEA CHANGE

Chinese policymakers deny that their country is a revisionist power. They claim that China seeks merely to defend a regional status quo that the United States is threatening. After all, they argue, China's claims to many of the region's disputed islands date back centuries. For example, Yang Yanyi, China's ambassador to the European Union, wrote in a 2016 op-ed that China has enjoyed "sovereignty over the

South China Sea Island . . . and the adjacent waters since ancient times." Chinese policymakers point out that the "nine-dash line," a demarcation of Chinese claims that runs along the edge of the South China Sea, has appeared on Chinese maps since the 1940s. "China's relevant claims have never exceeded the scope of the current international order," China's ambassador to the United Kingdom, Liu Xiaoming, argued in a 2016 speech criticizing the decision by an international tribunal in The Hague to rule against China in the South China Sea dispute. "China's rejection of the arbitration is to uphold the postwar international order," he said. According to Beijing, the South China Sea has always been, and will always be, Chinese territory; China, in other words, remains a status quo power, not a revisionist one.

But even if its territorial claims are not new, China rarely sought to enforce them until recently. For the past few years, however, China has grown increasingly assertive in its territorial disputes. In 2012, to the dismay of Tokyo and Washington, Beijing declared an "air defense identification zone" over the Senkaku Islands (known in China as the Diaoyu Islands), which are currently controlled by Japan but which China also claims, requiring aircraft flying through the zone to identify themselves to Chinese authorities. That same year, China maneuvered the Philippines out of Scarborough Shoal—a reef just over 100 miles from the Philippines and more than 500 miles from China. Today, its navy, coast guard, and "maritime militia" of fishing boats deny Philippine vessels access to the area. Meanwhile, China has presided over an extraordinary construction project in the South China Sea, building a string of artificial islands. As the Asia Maritime Transparency Initiative, a website that monitors activity in the disputed territory, has noted, "The number, size, and construction make it clear these are for military purposes—and they are the smoking gun that shows China has every intention of militarizing the Spratly Islands," a contested archipelago. China has drilled for oil in the waters of the contested Paracel Islands, ignoring Vietnamese protests and keeping Vietnamese ships away from the area. Last year, China sent a swarm of approximately 230 fishing boats, escorted by coast guard ships, into the waters around the Diaoyu/Senkaku Islands, and it has also escalated the situation by sending more powerful military forces into the area, such as a frigate and an air force bomber.

China is not the only revisionist power in the U.S.-Chinese relationship.

What's more, over the past few years, China has modernized its military. According to Captain James Fanell, the former chief of intelligence for the U.S. Pacific Fleet, China is building coast guard vessels "at an astonishing rate," some of which are among the largest coast guard ships in the world. China is also improving its conventional ballistic missiles, which threaten U.S. air bases and ports in the region, including Andersen Air Force Base, on Guam, a crucial U.S. military hub. These moves jeopardize the entire U.S. strategy for projecting power in East Asia.

In the eyes of all but Beijing, this clearly counts as revisionist behavior. And it has touched off a flurry of activity among countries that feel threatened. The Philippines, although possibly moving closer to China under President Rodrigo Duterte, has challenged China's territorial claims in an international tribunal. Australia has strengthened its military and deepened its alliance with the United States. Singapore, not a U.S. treaty ally but a longtime U.S. partner, has increased its defense spending and has begun to work more closely with the U.S. Navy. Despite the legacy of the Vietnam War, Hanoi and Washington have begun to move toward closer security cooperation.

Chinese behavior has also shocked Japan into action. Japanese leaders have rejected military statecraft for more than half a century. But under Prime Minister Shinzo Abe, Japan has reinterpreted (and may eventually revise) its constitution to permit more military activism and is forging closer ties with other countries worried about Chinese revisionism, including Australia and India.

A Taiwanese Coast Guard patrol ship near the coast of Itu Aba, which the Taiwanese call Taiping, in the South China Sea, November 2016.

So far, Japan's response to China has been restrained. Although changes in the Japanese defense posture often generate alarmist headlines, Japan's actions to date have been modest, especially when compared with how great powers normally behave when confronted by a rising power in their neighborhood. The Japanese public is preoccupied with a lagging economy and an aging society; it has no interest in military statecraft and has disapproved of the security reforms pushed by Abe and other conservatives. But as the world's third-largest economy, Japan has tremendous latent power; a sufficiently alarmed Tokyo could decide to increase its military spending from the current one percent of GDP to two or three percent—an undesirable outcome for Beijing.

Chinese officials argue that U.S. interference has caused its neighbors to respond with alarm, but China's own revisionism is to blame. Consider that for the past 60 years, even as Washington constantly entreated Japan to play a more active military role in the U.S.-Japanese alliance, Tokyo stepped up only when it felt threatened, as it did in the late 1970s when the Soviet Union launched a military buildup in Asia. Today, Japan is responding not to U.S. pressure but to Chinese assertiveness. Beijing must understand how threatening its actions appear if it wishes to successfully manage its relations with its neighbors and with Washington.

POT, MEET KETTLE

Like their Chinese counterparts, U.S. foreign policy officials argue that the United States seeks merely to uphold the status quo in East Asia. They want to maintain military predominance in the region through the policy of a "rebalance" to Asia, prevent a return to an era when countries settled disputes unilaterally and by force, and support freedom of navigation and the law of the sea.

In its desire to preserve the current global economic system and its network of military alliances, the United States does favor the status quo. But at its heart, U.S. grand strategy seeks to spread liberalism and U.S. influence. The goal, in other words, is not preservation but transformation.

After World War II, the United States formed a network of partners, supported by military alliances and international institutions, and sought to expand it. Prosperity and peace, created through trade and institutions, would prevail among the members of the liberal zone. As democracy and economic interdependence deepened, and as the zone widened, war would become less likely and respect for human rights would spread. Washington sought to pull countries into its orbit, regardless of whether they accepted its values. In time, perhaps engagement with the United States and with the liberal order would encourage the spread of liberalism to those countries, too. "The West was not just a geographical region with fixed borders," the scholar G. John Ikenberry has written. "Rather, it was an idea—a universal organizational form that could expand outward, driven by the spread of liberal democratic government and principles of conduct."

The strategy, to be sure, had elements of self-interest: Washington sought to create a liberal order that it itself led. But it also had a more revolutionary goal: the transformation of anarchy into order.

The United States has pursued this transformational grand strategy all over the world. In Europe, after the collapse of the Soviet Union in 1991, the United States and its allies did not preserve the status quo. Instead, they pushed eastward, enlarging NATO to absorb all of the Soviet Union's former Warsaw Pact allies and some former Soviet territories, such as the Baltic states. At the same time, the European Union expanded into eastern Europe. In Ukraine, U.S. and European policymakers encouraged the overthrow of a pro-Russian government in 2014 and helped install a Western-leaning one.

In the Middle East, U.S. policymakers saw the 2003 invasion of Iraq as an opportunity to advance democracy in the region. During the Arab Spring, they viewed the uprising in Libya as another chance to replace an anti-American dictator, and they encouraged the spread of democracy elsewhere as well. Underlying the United States' recent engagement with Iran is a desire to promote liberalization there, too.

The United States can encourage liberalism while acknowledging that its grand strategy appears deeply threatening to outsiders.

In East Asia, the United States has not only maintained and strengthened its longtime alliances with Australia, Japan, and the Philippines but also courted new partners, such as Malaysia and Singapore. And with its policy toward Vietnam, the United States may encourage a dramatic change in the regional status quo. Historically, Vietnam, which borders China, has fallen within its larger neighbor's sphere of influence, and since the Vietnam War, its relations with the United States have been bitter. In the past few years, however, Vietnam and the United States have deepened their economic ties, resolved previous disputes, and even explored greater security cooperation. Vietnam is also expanding its military ties with U.S. allies—namely, Australia, Japan, and the Philippines.

In each of these regions, U.S. diplomatic, economic, and military policies are aimed not at preserving but at transforming the status quo. "A country is one of three colors: blue, red, or gray," the Japanese journalist Hiroyuki Akita said in 2014 at a talk at the Sasakawa Peace Foundation, in Tokyo. "China wants to turn the gray countries red. The Americans and Japanese want to turn the gray countries blue." No one, in other words, is trying to preserve the status quo. U.S. foreign policy elites might object to Akita's blunt assessment and often dismiss the notion of "spheres of influence" as outdated, Cold War–era thinking. But the U.S. goal is to replace the old-fashioned competition for spheres of influence with a single liberal sphere led by the United States.

IN OR OUT?

China, of course, does not stand entirely outside the liberal international system. China has become the world's second-largest economy in large part by embracing some features of liberalism: it is now a top trading partner of many countries, including, of course, the United States. And China has gained greater influence in institutions such as the International Monetary Fund and the World Bank. The country both profits from and—increasingly, by virtue of its wealth, talent, and expertise—contributes to the liberal order.

Yet in several key respects, China remains outside that order. Its military modernization and regional assertiveness challenge U.S. primacy in Asia and the principle that countries should resolve territorial disputes through peaceful adjudication. Although China has introduced significant economic reforms, many observers question its support for liberal economic development. Beijing argues that the Asian Infrastructure Investment Bank, a Chinese-led international development bank, will uphold good governance and environmental protection. Yet Beijing could well renege on those promises.

China is clearly an outsider in the realm of human rights. The Chinese Communist Party maintains its grip on power through the threat and use of force. It harasses, arrests, and tortures political activists and suspected enemies, and it represses secessionist groups, such as the Mongolians, the Tibetans, and the Uighurs. Under Xi, the government has cracked down even more harshly on domestic dissent. As a 2015 Human Rights Watch report put it, the Chinese leader has "unleashed an extraordinary assault on basic human rights and their defenders with a ferocity unseen in recent years"; in 2016, the nongovernmental organization declared that "the trend for human rights . . . continued in a decidedly negative direction."

China also obstructs its liberal partners' efforts to promote human rights across the globe. In the 1990s, for example, China opposed UN intervention in Bosnia and Kosovo, arguing that the West should respect national sovereignty. And regarding Syria, China has vetoed multiple UN Security Council resolutions calling for a political solution.

U.S. President Barack Obama smiles as he attends a town hall meeting in Ho Chi Minh City, Vietnam, May 2016.

For illiberal countries, the inherently transformational nature of U.S. grand strategy appears deeply threatening—something U.S. foreign policy elites too often fail to recognize. NATO expansion, for example, provoked deep consternation in Moscow. As the political scientist Joshua Itzkowitz Shifrinson has noted, "Western scholars and policymakers should not be surprised that contemporary Russian leaders resent the United States' post–Cold War efforts and are willing to prevent further NATO expansion—by force, if necessary." U.S. and European efforts to encourage Ukraine to join NATO and the EU menaced Russia, and Russian President Vladimir Putin lashed out. This is not to excuse Putin's military aggression; he had other choices. But NATO members' inability to see how the expansion of their alliance threatened Russia represented a serious failure of strategic empathy.

In East Asia, adding Vietnam to the list of U.S. regional partners—or even allies—would seem to follow naturally from a strategy of spreading democracy and free markets and might insulate a liberalizing Vietnam from the coercive influence of its powerful neighbor. But a U.S. alliance with Vietnam would represent a dramatic departure from the status quo, and China would see it as such. U.S. foreign policy analysts sometimes invoke the benefits of closer U.S. relations with Hanoi without mentioning how threatening this development would appear to Beijing, which could react in a similar way toward Vietnam as Russia did toward Ukraine. U.S. policymakers should not automatically defer to China and Russia. But to understand the real tradeoffs of a given policy, they need to take into account how these great powers will likely react.

A BULL IN A CHINA SHOP?

One can argue that the United States' transformational strategy has had, and will continue to have, a profoundly positive effect on the world. Or one can argue that it is simply a manifestation of self-interested U.S. expansionism. It's hard to argue, however, that U.S. policy has sought to support the status quo.

Proponents of the post–World War II U.S. grand strategy might argue that there is no reason to adjust it now. They might insist that challenges from China and Russia demand, if anything, a stronger U.S. commitment to spreading liberalism. According to this view, the United States should strengthen its security commitments in eastern Europe and extend new ones there. In Asia, the United States should strengthen its existing alliances, align itself more closely with Vietnam, and clarify its commitment to defend Taiwan.

China, unlike the Soviet Union, does not have a revolutionary ideology.

By contrast, realist critics might caution that as the global balance of power changes, so must U.S. grand strategy. A transformational approach may have made sense in the 1990s: it allowed the United States and its liberal partners to gain ground when China and Russia posed little threat. Today, however, China's rise and Russia's resurgence make this strategy too provocative. In this view, Washington must be wary of a growing risk of great-power conflict and, because all three countries possess nuclear weapons, potentially catastrophic escalation. These critics would have Washington prioritize great-power stability over its transformational goals.

The best way forward is a compromise between the approach of the liberal internationalists and that of the realists. Washington should continue to look for opportunities to promote liberalism, but it should do so through less threatening policies and in regions where its actions are less likely to have strategic repercussions for U.S. relationships with some of the world's most powerful countries. For example, the United States can support the building of institutions and civil society in Africa, Latin America, and parts of Asia and the Middle East without threatening the core interests of other great powers. U.S. policymakers should be wary of extending alliances to the borders of China or Russia or attempting to advance democracy within those countries. The United States can encourage liberalism while acknowledging that its grand strategy appears deeply threatening to outsiders.

If Hillary Clinton, the Democratic nominee, had won the presidential election, the United States would probably have continued to pursue its transformational strategy. It is much less clear, however, how Trump's presidency will shape U.S. grand strategy and U.S.-Chinese relations. On the one hand, the Trump administration could prove deeply destabilizing. Trump's phone call with the Taiwanese president, for example, has introduced real uncertainty about U.S. policy toward Taiwan, potentially shattering a delicate compromise that has held for four decades. If the Trump administration pokes sticks into more areas where previous U.S. and Chinese governments have forged compromises, it will preside over a deterioration of an already troubled relationship.

But Trump could also reduce tensions if he proves less assertive about promoting liberalism than the liberal internationalists who have presided over U.S. foreign policy since the end of the Cold War. Although Trump has not outlined his views on grand strategy, he seems less concerned with transforming the world's political system and more interested in making good bilateral deals for the United States. So Trump, caring little about promoting further liberalization in Asia, might dismiss an alliance with Vietnam, a weak nation embroiled in a territorial dispute with a great power, as a bad deal. If Trump's pragmatism makes him more willing than liberal internationalists to compromise, his leadership could prove stabilizing in this respect.

For years, foreign policy analysts in the United States, Japan, and Europe took heart from at least one reassuring factor in U.S.-Chinese relations: China, unlike the Soviet Union, does not have a revolutionary ideology. Beijing has not tried to export an ideology around the world.

Washington has. In attempting to transform anarchy into liberal order, the United States has pursued an idealistic, visionary, and in many ways laudable goal. Yet its audacity terrifies those on the outside. The United States and its partners need not necessarily defer to that fear—but they must understand it.

JENNIFER LIND is Associate Professor of Government at Dartmouth College. Follow her on Twitter @profLind.

© Foreign Affairs

A Vision of Trump at War

How the President Could Stumble Into Conflict

Philip Gordon

Let's get ready to rumble: a rally in Pyongyang, January 2016

Just a few months into the Trump administration, it still isn't clear what course the president's foreign policy will ultimately take. What is clear, however, is that the impulsiveness, combativeness, and recklessness that characterized Donald Trump's election campaign have survived the transition into the presidency. Since taking office, Trump has continued to challenge accepted norms, break with diplomatic traditions, and respond to perceived slights or provocations with insults or threats of his own. The core of his foreign policy message is that the United States will no longer allow itself to be taken advantage of by friends or foes abroad. After decades of "losing" to other countries, he says he is going to put "America first" and start winning again.

It could be that Trump is simply staking out tough bargaining positions as a tactical matter, the approach to negotiations he has famously called "the art of the deal." President Richard Nixon long ago developed the "madman theory," the idea that he could frighten his adversaries into believing he was so volatile he might do something crazy if they failed to meet his demands—a tactic that Trump, whose reputation for volatility is firmly established, seems particularly well suited to employ.

The problem, however, is that negotiations sometimes fail, and adversaries are themselves often brazen and unpredictable. After all, Nixon's madman theory—designed to force the North Vietnamese to compromise—did not work. Moreover, putting the theory into practice requires the capacity to act judiciously at the appropriate moment, something that Trump, as president, has yet to demonstrate. And whereas a failed business deal allows both parties to walk away unscathed if disappointed, a failed diplomatic gambit can lead to political instability, costly trade disputes, the proliferation of dangerous weapons, or even war. History is littered with examples of leaders who, like Trump, came to power fueled by a sense of national grievance and promises to force adversaries into submission, only to end up mired in a military, diplomatic, or economic conflict they would come to regret.

Will that happen to Trump? Nobody knows. But what if one could? What if, like Ebenezer Scrooge in Charles Dickens' A Christmas Carol, Trump could meet a ghost from the future offering a vision of where his policies might lead by the end of his term before he decides on them at its start?

The problem is that negotiations sometimes fail, and adversaries are themselves often brazen and unpredictable.

It is possible that such a ghost would show him a version of the future in which his administration, after a turbulent start, moderated over time, proved more conventional than predicted, and even had some success in negotiating, as he has pledged, "better deals." But there is a real risk that events will turn out far worse—a future in which Trump's erratic style and confrontational policies destroy an already fragile world order and lead to open conflict—in the most likely cases, with Iran, China, or North Korea.

In the narratives that follow, everything described as having taken place before mid-March 2017 actually happened. That which takes place after that date is—at least at the time of publication—fiction.

STUMBLING INTO WAR WITH IRAN

It is September 2017, and the White House is consumed with a debate about options for escalation with Iran. Another dozen Americans have been killed in an Iranian-sponsored attack on U.S. soldiers in Iraq, and the president is frustrated that previous air strikes in Iran failed to deter this sort of deadly aggression. He is tempted to retaliate much more aggressively this time but also knows that doing so risks involving U.S. troops even further in what is already a costly and unpopular war—the very sort of "mess" he had promised to avoid. Looking back, he now sees that this conflict probably became inevitable when he named his foreign policy team and first started to implement his new approach toward Iran.

Well before his election, of course, Trump had criticized the Iran nuclear agreement as "the worst deal ever negotiated" and promised to put a stop to Iran's "aggressive push to destabilize and dominate" the Middle East. Some of his top advisers were deeply hostile to Iran and known to favor a more confrontational approach, including his first national security adviser, Michael Flynn; his CIA director, Mike Pompeo; his chief strategist, Steve Bannon; and his defense secretary, James Mattis. Some of Mattis' former military colleagues said he had a 30-year-long obsession with Iran, noting, as one marine told Politico, "It's almost like he wants to get even with them."

During his campaign and first months in office, Trump whipped up anti-Iranian feelings and consistently misled the public about what the nuclear deal entailed. He falsely insisted that the United States "received absolutely nothing" from it, that it permitted Iran to eventually get the bomb, and that it gave $150 billion to Iran (apparently referring to a provision of the deal that allowed Iran to access some $50 billion of its own money that had been frozen in foreign accounts). Critics claimed that the rhetoric was reminiscent of the Bush administration's exaggerations of Iraq's weapons of mass destruction programs in the run-up to the Iraq war. In February 2017, in response to an Iranian ballistic missile test, Flynn brashly declared that he was "officially putting Iran on notice." Two days later, the administration announced a range of new sanctions on 25 Iranian individuals and companies involved in the ballistic missile program.

Trump whipped up anti-Iranian feelings and consistently misled the public about what the nuclear deal entailed.

Perhaps just as predictably, Iran dismissed the administration's tough talk. It continued to test its missiles, insisting that neither the nuclear deal nor UN Security Council resolutions prohibited it from doing so. Ali Khamenei, Iran's supreme leader, even taunted Trump for his controversial immigration and travel ban, thanking him on Twitter for revealing the "true face" of the United States.

Tehran also continued its policy of shipping arms to the Houthi rebels in Yemen and providing military assistance to Bashar al-Assad's regime in Syria, neither of which proved particularly costly to the Iranian treasury. U.S. efforts to get Russia to limit Iran's role in Syria were ignored, adding to the White House's frustration.

To the surprise of many, growing U.S. pressure on Iran did not immediately lead to the collapse of the nuclear deal. As soon as he took office, Trump ended the Obama administration's practice of encouraging banks and international companies to ensure that Iran benefited economically from the deal. And he expressed support for congressional plans to sanction additional Iranian entities for terrorism or human rights violations, as top officials insisted was permitted by the nuclear deal. Iran complained that these "backdoor" sanctions would violate the agreement yet took no action. By March 2017, U.S. officials were concluding internally—and some of the administration's supporters began to gloat—that Trump's tougher approach was succeeding.

Iranian ships take part in naval war game in the Persian Gulf and the Strait of Hormuz in April 2010.

Different behavior on either side could have prevented relations from deteriorating. But ultimately, the deal could not be sustained. In the early summer of 2017, real signs of trouble started to emerge. Under pressure from hardline factions within Iran, which had their own interest in spiking the deal, Tehran had continued its provocative behavior, including the unjustified detention of dual U.S.-Iranian citizens, throughout the spring. In June, after completing a review of his Iran policy, Trump put Iran's Islamic Revolutionary Guard Corps on the State Department's list of foreign terrorist organizations and announced that continued sanctions relief would be contingent on Iran's release of all U.S. detainees and a return to negotiations to address the nuclear deal's "flaws." Instead of submitting to these demands, Iran responded with defiance. Its new president, a hard-liner who had defeated Hassan Rouhani in the May 2017 election, declared that in the face of U.S. "noncompliance," Iran would resume certain prohibited nuclear activities, including testing advanced centrifuges and expanding its stockpile of low-enriched uranium. Washington was suddenly abuzz with talk of the need for a new effort to choke off Iran economically or even a preventive military strike.

The Trump administration had been confident that other countries would back its tougher approach and had warned allies and adversaries alike that they must choose between doing business with Iran and doing business with the United States. But the pressure did not work as planned. China, France, Germany, India, Japan, Russia, South Korea, and the United Kingdom all said that the deal had been working before the United States sought to renegotiate it, and they blamed Washington for precipitating the crisis. The EU even passed legislation making it illegal for European companies to cooperate with U.S. secondary sanctions. Trump fumed and vowed they would pay for their betrayal.

As the United States feuded with its closest partners, tensions with Iran escalated further. Frustrated by continued Iranian support for the Houthi rebels in Yemen, the Pentagon stepped up patrols in the Strait of Hormuz and loosened the rules of engagement for U.S. forces. When an Iranian patrol boat aggressively approached a U.S. cruiser, in circumstances that are still disputed, the U.S. ship responded with deadly defensive force, killing 25 Iranian sailors.

The outrage in Iran bolstered support for the regime and led to widespread calls for revenge, which the country's new president could not resist. Less than a week later, the Iranian-backed militia group Kataib Hezbollah killed six U.S. soldiers in Iraq. With the American public demanding retaliation, some called for diplomacy, recalling how, in January 2016, U.S. Secretary of State John Kerry and Iranian Foreign Minister Mohammad Javad Zarif spoke directly to defuse the situation after U.S. sailors drifted into Iranian waters. This time, the EU offered to mediate the crisis.

But the administration wanted nothing to do with what it considered the Obama administration's humiliating appeasement of Iran. Instead, to teach Iran a lesson, Trump authorized a cruise missile strike on a known Islamic Revolutionary Guard Corps intelligence headquarters, destroying three buildings and killing a dozen officers and an unknown number of civilians.

Trump's advisers predicted that Iran would back down, but as nationalist fervor grew in Iran, Tehran escalated the conflict, calculating that the American public had no desire to spend more blood or treasure in the Middle East. Kataib Hezbollah and other Shiite militias in Iraq, some directed by Iran and others acting independently, launched further attacks on U.S. personnel. Tehran forced the weak government in Baghdad to demand the Americans' departure from Iraq, which would deal a huge blow to the U.S.-led campaign against the Islamic State, or ISIS.

As Washington reimposed the sanctions that had been suspended by the nuclear deal, Iran abandoned the limits on its enrichment of uranium, expelled the UN monitors, and announced that it was no longer bound by the agreement. With the CIA concluding that Iran was now back on the path to a nuclear weapons capability, Trump's top advisers briefed the president in the Oval Office. Some counseled restraint, but others, led by Bannon and Mattis, insisted that the only credible option was to destroy the Iranian nuclear infrastructure with a massive preventive strike, while reinforcing the U.S. presence in Iraq to deal with the likely Iranian retaliation. Pompeo, a longstanding advocate of regime change in Iran, argued that such a strike might also lead to a popular uprising and the ousting of the supreme leader, an encouraging notion that Trump himself had heard think-tank experts endorse on television.

Once again, nervous allies stepped in and tried to broker a diplomatic solution. They tried to put the 2015 nuclear deal back in place, arguing that it now looked attractive by comparison. But it was too late. U.S. strikes on Iran's nuclear facilities in Arak, Fordow, Isfahan, Natanz, and Parchin led to retaliatory counterstrikes against U.S. forces in Iraq, U.S. retaliation against targets in Iran, terrorist attacks against Americans in Europe and the Middle East, and vows from Tehran to rebuild its nuclear program bigger and better than before. The president who had vowed to stop squandering American lives and resources in the Middle East now found himself wondering how he had ended up at war there.

FIGHTING CHINA

JERRY LAMPEN / REUTERS

China's national flag is raised during the opening ceremony of the Beijing 2008 Olympic Games at the Bird's Nest Stadium, August 2008.

It is October 2017, and experts are calling it the most dangerous confrontation between nuclear powers since the Cuban missile crisis. After a U.S.-Chinese trade war escalated well beyond what either side had predicted, a clash in the South China Sea has led to casualties on both sides and heavy exchanges of fire between the U.S. and Chinese navies. There are rumors that China has placed its nuclear forces on high alert. The conflict that so many long feared has begun.

Of the many foreign targets of Trump's withering criticism during the campaign and the early months of his presidency, China topped the list. As a candidate, Trump repeatedly accused the country of destroying American jobs and stealing U.S. secrets. "We can't continue to allow China to rape our country," he said. Bannon, who early in the administration set up a shadow national security council in the White House, had even predicted conflict with China. "We're going to war in the

South China Sea in five to ten years," he said in March 2016. "There's no doubt about that."

Not long after the election, Trump took a congratulatory phone call from Taiwanese President Tsai Ing-wen, breaking with decades of diplomatic tradition and suggesting a potential change in the United States' "one China" policy. It wasn't clear whether the move was inadvertent or deliberate, but either way, Trump defended his approach and insisted that the policy was up for negotiation unless China made concessions on trade. "Did China ask us if it was OK to devalue their currency (making it hard for our companies to compete), heavily tax our products going into their country (the U.S. doesn't tax them) or to build a massive military complex in the middle of the South China Sea?" he tweeted. "I don't think so!" In February 2017, after a call with Chinese President Xi Jinping, Trump announced that the United States would honor the "one China" policy after all. Asia experts were relieved, but it must have infuriated the president that so many thought he had backed down. "Trump lost his first fight with Xi and he will be looked at as a paper tiger," Shi Yinhong, a professor at Renmin University of China, told The New York Times.

There were other early warning signs of the clashes to come. At his confirmation hearings for secretary of state, Rex Tillerson appeared to draw a new redline in the South China Sea, noting that China's access to islands there "is not going to be allowed." Some dismissed the statement as overblown rhetoric, but Beijing did not. The state-run China Daily warned that any attempt to enforce such a policy could lead to a "devastating confrontation," and the Global Times said it could lead to "large-scale war."

Then there were the disputes about trade. To head the new White House National Trade Council, Trump nominated Peter Navarro, the author of The Coming China Wars, Death by

China, and other provocative books that describe U.S. Chinese relations in zero-sum terms and argue for increased U.S. tariffs and trade sanctions. Like Bannon, Navarro regularly invoked the specter of military conflict with Beijing, and he argued that tougher economic measures were necessary not only to rectify the U.S.-Chinese trade balance but also to weaken China's military power, which he claimed would inevitably be used against the United States. The early rhetoric worried many observers, but they took solace in the idea that neither side could afford a confrontation.

It was the decisions that followed that made war all but inevitable. In June 2017, when North Korea tested yet another long-range missile, which brought it closer to having the ability to strike the United States, Trump demanded that China check its small ally and announced "serious consequences" if it refused. China had no interest in promoting North Korea's nuclear capacity, but it worried that completely isolating Pyongyang, as Trump was demanding, could cause the regime to collapse—sending millions of poor North Korean refugees streaming into China and leaving behind a united Korea ruled by Seoul, armed with North Korea's nuclear weapons, and allied with Washington. China agreed to another UN Security Council statement condemning North Korea and extended a suspension of coal imports from the country but refused to take further action. Angry about Trump's incessant criticism and confrontation over trade, Xi saw the United States as a greater danger to China than North Korea was and said he refused to be bullied by Washington.

At the same time, the U.S. current account deficit with China had swelled, driven in part by the growing U.S. budget deficits that resulted from Trump's massive tax cuts. That, combined with Chinese intransigence over North Korea, convinced the White House that it was time to get tough. Outside experts, along with Trump's own secretary of state and secretary of the treasury, cautioned against the risks of a dangerous escalation, but the president dismissed their hand-wringing and said that the days of letting China take advantage of Americans were over. In July, the administration formally branded China a "currency manipulator" (despite evidence that it had actually been spending its currency reserves to uphold the value of the yuan) and imposed a 45 percent tariff on Chinese imports. To the delight of the crowd at a campaign-style rally in Florida, Trump announced that these new measures would remain in place until China boosted the value of its currency, bought more U.S. goods, and imposed tougher sanctions on North Korea.

The president's more hawkish advisers assured him that China's response would prove limited, given its dependence on exports and its massive holdings of U.S. Treasury bonds. But they underestimated the intense nationalism that the U.S. actions had stoked. Xi had to show strength, and he hit back.

All Trump wanted to do was get a better deal from China.

Within days, Xi announced that China was taking the United States to the World Trade Organization over the import tariff (a case he felt certain China would win) and imposed a 45 percent countertariff on U.S. imports. The Chinese believed that the reciprocal tariffs would hurt the United States more than China (since Americans bought far more Chinese goods than the other way around) and knew that the resulting inflation—especially for goods such as clothing, shoes, toys, and electronics—would hurt Trump's blue-collar constituency. Even more important, they felt they were more willing to make sacrifices than the Americans were.

Xi also instructed China's central bank to sell $100 billion in U.S. Treasury bonds, a move that immediately drove up U.S. interest rates and knocked 800 points off the Dow Jones industrial average in a single day. That China started using some of the cash resulting from the sales to buy large stakes in major U.S. companies at depressed prices only fueled a nationalist reaction in the United States. Trump tapped into it, calling for a new law to block Chinese investment.

With personal insults flying back and forth across the Pacific, Trump announced that if China did not start treating the United States fairly, Washington might reconsider the "one China" policy after all. Encouraged by Bannon, who argued privately that it was better to have the inevitable confrontation with China while the United States still enjoyed military superiority, Trump speculated publicly about inviting the president of Taiwan to the White House and selling new antimissile systems and submarines to the island.

China responded that any change in U.S. policy toward Taiwan would be met with an "overwhelming response," which experts interpreted to mean at a minimum cutting off trade with Taiwan (which sends 30 percent of its exports to China) and at a maximum military strikes against targets on the island. With over one billion Chinese on the mainland passionately committed to the country's nominal unity, few doubted that Beijing meant what it said. On October 1, China's normally tepid National Day celebrations turned into a frightening display of anti-Americanism.

It was in this environment that an incident in the South China Sea led to the escalation so many had feared. The details remain murky, but it was triggered when a U.S. surveillance ship operating in disputed waters in heavy fog accidentally rammed a Chinese trawler that was harassing it. In the confusion that ensued, a People's Liberation Army Navy frigate fired on the unarmed U.S. ship, a U.S. destroyer sank the Chinese frigate, and a Chinese torpedo struck and badly damaged the destroyer, killing three Americans.

A U.S. aircraft carrier task force is being rushed to the region, and China has deployed additional attack submarines there and begun aggressive overflights and patrols throughout the South China Sea. Tillerson is seeking to reach his Chinese counterpart, but officials in Beijing wonder whether he even speaks for the administration and fear

Trump will accept nothing short of victory. Leaked U.S. intelligence estimates suggest that a large-scale conflict could quickly lead to hundreds of thousands of casualties, draw in neighboring states, and destroy trillions of dollars' worth of economic output. But with nationalism raging in both countries, neither capital sees a way to back down. All Trump wanted to do was get a better deal from China.

DAMIR SAGOLJ / REUTERS

During the military parade marking the 70th anniversary of the end of World War II in Beijing, China, September 2015.

THE NEXT KOREAN WAR

It is December 2018, and North Korea has just launched a heavy artillery barrage against targets in Seoul, killing thousands, or perhaps tens of thousands; it is too soon to say. U.S. and South Korean forces—now unified under U.S. command, according to the provisions of the Mutual Defense Treaty—have fired artillery and rockets at North Korea's military positions and launched air strikes against its advanced air defense network. From a bunker somewhere near Pyongyang, the country's erratic dictator, Kim Jong Un, has issued a statement promising to "burn Seoul and Tokyo to the ground"—a reference to North Korea's stockpile of nuclear and chemical weapons— if the "imperialist" forces do not immediately cease their attacks.

Even Trump's harshest critics acknowledge that the United States had no good choices in North Korea.

Washington had expected some sort of a North Korean response when it preemptively struck the test launch of an intercontinental ballistic missile capable of delivering a nuclear warhead to the continental United States, fulfilling Trump's pledge to prevent Pyongyang from acquiring that ability. But few thought North Korea would go so far as to risk its own destruction by attacking South Korea. Now, Trump must decide whether to continue with the war and risk nuclear escalation—or accept what will be seen as a humiliating retreat. Some of his advisers are urging him to quickly finish the job, whereas others warn that doing so would cost the lives of too many of the 28,000 U.S. soldiers stationed on the peninsula, to say nothing of the ten million residents of Seoul. Assembled in the White House Situation Room, Trump and his aides ponder their terrible options.

How did it come to this? Even Trump's harshest critics acknowledge that the United States had no good choices in North Korea. For more than 20 years, the paranoid, isolated regime in Pyongyang had developed its nuclear and missile capabilities and seemed impervious to incentives and disincentives alike. The so-called Agreed Framework, a 1994 deal to halt North Korea's nuclear program, fell apart in 2003 when Pyongyang was caught violating it, leading the George W. Bush administration to abandon the deal in favor of tougher sanctions. Multiple rounds of talks since then produced little progress. By 2017, experts estimated that North Korea possessed more than a dozen nuclear warheads and was stockpiling the material for more. They also thought North Korea had missiles capable of delivering those warheads to targets throughout Asia and was testing missiles that could give it the capacity to strike the West Coast of the United States by 2023.

Early in the administration, numerous outside experts and former senior officials urged Trump to make North Korea a top priority. Accepting that total dismantlement of the country's nuclear and missile programs was not a realistic nearterm goal, most called for negotiations that would offer a package of economic incentives and security assurances in exchange for a halt to further testing and development. A critical component, they argued, would be outreach to China, the only country that might be able to influence North Korea.

But the administration preferred a more confrontational approach. Even before Trump took office, when Kim blustered about developing the capacity to strike the United States with a nuclear weapon, Trump responded on Twitter: "It won't happen!" On February 12, 2017, North Korea fired a test missile 310 miles into the Sea of Japan at the very moment Trump was meeting with Japanese Prime Minister Shinzo Abe at his Mar-a-Lago estate, in Florida. The next morning, Stephen Miller, a senior adviser to Trump, announced that the United States would soon be sending a signal to North Korea in the form of a major military buildup that would show "unquestioned military strength beyond anything anyone can imagine." Later that month, Trump announced plans for a $54 billion increase in U.S. defense spending for 2018, with corresponding cuts in the budget for diplomacy. And in March 2017,

Tillerson traveled to Asia and declared that "the political and diplomatic efforts of the past 20 years" had failed and that a "new approach" was needed.

In the ensuing months, critics urged the administration to accompany its military buildup with regional diplomacy, but Trump chose otherwise. He made clear that U.S. foreign policy had changed. Unlike what his predecessor had done with Iran, he said, he was not going to reward bad behavior. Instead, the administration announced in the summer of 2018 that North Korea was "officially on notice." Although the White House agreed with critics that the best way to pressure North Korea was through China, it proved impossible to cooperate with Beijing while erecting tariffs and attacking it for "raping" the United States economically.

Thus did the problem grow during the administration's first two years. North Korea continued to test missiles and develop fissile material. It occasionally incited South Korea, launching shells across the demilitarized zone and provoking some near misses at sea. The war of words between Pyongyang and Washington also escalated—advisers could not get the president to bite his tongue in response to Kim's outrageous taunts—and Trump repeated in even more colorful language his Twitter warning that he would not allow Pyongyang to test a nuclear-capable missile that could reach the United States.

When the intelligence community picked up signs that Pyongyang was about to do so, the National Security Council met, and the chairman of the Joint Chiefs of Staff briefed the president on his options. He could try to shoot down the test missile in flight, but shooting carried a high risk of missing, and even a successful intercept might provoke a military response. He could do nothing, but that would mean losing face and emboldening North Korea. Or he could destroy the test missile on its launch pad with a barrage of cruise missiles, blocking Pyongyang's path to a nuclear deterrent, enforcing his redline, and sending a clear message to the rest of the world. Sources present at the meeting reported that when the president chose the third option, he said, "We have to start winning wars again."

LEARNING FROM THE FUTURE

These frightening futures are far from inevitable. Indeed, for all the early bluster and promises of a dramatic break with the past, U.S. foreign policy may well turn out to be not as revolutionary or reckless as many fear. Trump has already demonstrated his ability to reverse course without compunction on a multitude of issues, from abortion to the Iraq war, and sound advice from some of his more seasoned advisers could moderate his potential for rash behavior.

On the other hand, given what we have seen so far of the president's temperament, decision-making style, and foreign policy, these visions of what might lie ahead are hardly implausible: foreign policy disasters do happen. Imagine if a ghost from the future could have given world leaders in 1914 a glimpse of the cataclysm their policies would produce. Or if in 1965, U.S. President Lyndon Johnson could have seen what escalation in Vietnam would lead to a decade later. Or if in 2003, U.S. President George W. Bush could have been shown a preview of the results of the invasion of Iraq. In each case, unwise decisions, a flawed process, and wishful thinking did lead to a catastrophe that could have been, and often was, predicted in advance.

Maybe Trump is right that a massive military buildup, a reputation for unpredictability, a high-stakes negotiating style, and a refusal to compromise will convince other countries to make concessions that will make America safe, prosperous, and great again. But then again, maybe he's wrong.

CORRECTION APPENDED (March 28, 2017)

An earlier version of this article overstated the link between growing U.S. budget deficits and the value of the dollar when discussing U.S. tensions with China. In fact, although growing budget deficits would likely lead to a growing current account deficit, they would not necessarily drive up the value of the dollar.

PHILIP GORDON is a Senior Fellow at the Council on Foreign Relations. From 2013 to 2015, he was Special Assistant to the President and White House Coordinator for the Middle East, North Africa, and the Gulf Region.

© Foreign Affairs

Intelligence and the Presidency

How to Get It Right

Jami Miscik

Truth tellers: at the headquarters of the CIA, in Virginia, August 2008.

U.S. presidents and other senior policymakers often come into office knowing little about the 17 federal agencies and offices that make up the U.S. intelligence community, but in short order, they come to rely heavily on its unique technologies, tradecraft, and expert analysis. The intelligence community's mission is to provide national leaders with the best and most timely information available on global affairs and national security issues—information that, in turn, can help those leaders achieve their foreign policy objectives.

The president is the country's top intelligence consumer and the only person who can authorize a covert action, and the services he receives from the intelligence community can be invaluable—providing early warning of brewing trouble, identifying and disrupting threats before they materialize, gaining insight into foreign leaders, and discreetly affecting developments abroad. For the relationship between intelligence producers and consumers to work effectively, however, each needs to understand and trust the other.

INFORMATION, NOT POLICY

The most common misperception about the intelligence community is that it makes policy. It doesn't. As Allen Dulles, the director of central intelligence from 1953 to 1961, once said, "Intelligence is the servant, not the master, of foreign policy." A new administration considers and articulates what it stands for and what it hopes to achieve; it develops policies and informational priorities, and then it deploys the resources of the intelligence community based on those priorities.

The intelligence community, in other words, cannot operate in a vacuum. It must be told what to look for and what is most important. The White House must be disciplined in its tasking; if everything is a priority, then nothing is. Moreover, it needs to remain engaged and update its thinking. Over time, some issues will rise in importance and some will fall. Without regular dialogue and guidance, the intelligence community will do what it can to respond appropriately to global changes and improvise ways to balance competing requests. But the tradeoffs will often go unnoticed by senior policymakers until a crisis exposes deficiencies in intelligence collection.

It is the essence of the intelligence community's creed to speak truth to power.

The intelligence community needs to have close and regular access to all senior national security policymakers, including the president, the vice president, the secretary of state, the secretary of defense, the secretary of homeland security, and the national security adviser. If the producers of intelligence don't know the status of ongoing operations and negotiations, then their product will not be responsive to the consumers' needs and will be dismissed as irrelevant. And the window of policy relevance is open only briefly. The reward for warning about something too early is to be ignored, and the reward for warning too late is to risk becoming the latest example of intelligence failure.

In order to work well together during a crisis, when the stakes are highest, intelligence producers and consumers need to have established a good working relationship long before the crisis hits. Personal connections and regular briefings can help establish trust and mutual understanding. Noncrisis periods are opportunities to work on the relationship and prepare for the future, because when a crisis does hit, there is no time for on-the-job training and coming up to speed on how to best utilize intelligence assets.

U.S. President Donald Trump at the Central Intelligence Agency in Langley, Virginia, United States, January 2017.

The intelligence community's relationship with senior policymakers must be close and trusted, or else neither party will be able to do its job well. At the same time, intelligence professionals have to be careful not to get drawn into policy debates or partisan politics. Should a president or a cabinet member ask intelligence officers for an opinion on policy, the officers should refuse to give it, because that is not their remit; they do not make policy. The training and culture of intelligence officers underscore this ethos.

The American system of government requires a new president to place his full trust in an intelligence community that loyally served his predecessor right up until the inauguration. This is a lot to ask, especially if senior administration figures have little experience with the intelligence community. The potential for distrust is high, but intelligence officers are loyal, trustworthy, and committed to serving the presidency. They serve without regard to political affiliation and are trained to present their findings without personal or political agendas.

Reading a report from a CIA officer in the field, a former White House official once asked, "Is he a Republican or a Democrat?" Not only did the briefer not know, but as would most of his colleagues, he found the very premise of the question abhorrent. The new administration should take care not to make assumptions about the political leanings of the intelligence community or infer that it knows how intelligence officers voted. Unlike in other U.S. government departments, where there are many political appointees, in the intelligence community, most members are careerists who have served under both Democratic and Republican administrations. The whole point of the National Security Act of 1947, which codified modern governmental arrangements, was to foster a professional national security community inoculated against partisan politics. This is why public concerns were raised when a political adviser was added to the National Security Council's Principals Committee.

When intelligence officers brief senior policymakers, they are there to do a job, not to be loved or to score political points. A former director of central intelligence likened it to being the skunk at the garden party: frequently, the job is to tell policymakers what they do not want to hear. Senior administration officials are invested in the policies of their administration, but intelligence officers are not. It is the essence of the intelligence community's creed to speak truth to power, and those who do so responsibly are considered heroes of the profession.

GREAT EXPECTATIONS

At the start of a new administration, policymakers should have realistic expectations of what intelligence can and cannot do. Many assume that the intelligence community tries to predict the future. It does not. Intelligence officers present the intelligence that has been collected, assess it, and evaluate possible actions and outcomes. They anticipate possible contingencies and warn about possible dangers, but they do not try to predict results. The relationship between intelligence officers and policymakers resembles that of scouts and coaches. A scout is responsible for studying the strengths, weaknesses, and tendencies of the other team. The scout's job is to provide data and insights on the opposition. Armed with that information, the coach can then decide how to deploy the team and what plays to execute. The scout's goal is to help the coach win, but nobody expects the scout to correctly predict the final score before the game is played.

The importance of the intelligence community's relationship with the president himself cannot be overstated.

Policymakers new to government must understand that intelligence operates in a world of uncertainties and changing realities. As Clausewitz noted, "Many intelligence reports in war are contradictory; even more are false, and most are uncertain.... In short, most intelligence is false." All too often, this remains true today. But false or incorrect is not fake, nor is it necessarily failure. Intelligence officers are forced to deal with partial bits of information, some sources who faithfully report inaccurate information that they mistakenly believe is correct, and other sources who are deliberately trying to mislead and deceive. Intelligence is cumulative, moreover, and earlier reports may prove less accurate than later ones. As more intelligence is collected, analysts can dismiss some reports that they had once credited. This natural and correct dynamic should not be seen as waffling or simply changing the story. It is actually how increasingly sophisticated answers to intelligence puzzles emerge.

When the intelligence community gets it wrong, it must own its mistakes. These professionals owe the country, the president, and themselves an understanding of what went wrong, why, and what measures have been taken to ensure the same mistakes are not repeated. That is exactly what I believed the CIA needed in the aftermath of the invasion of Iraq in 2003, when no stockpiles of weapons of mass destruction were found, completely contrary to our judgments. I put together a special team to find out where we had gone wrong, and then, borrowing a practice from the U.S. Navy, I ordered a "safety stand-down" for all the analysts at the CIA to ensure that the lessons learned were conveyed to everybody, not just those who had worked on Iraq. In a culture of secrets, some may try to gloss over problems in hopes that the mistakes are never discovered. It is incumbent on the leadership of the intelligence community to hold their officers accountable and demand that mistakes be acknowledged, analyzed, and rectified.

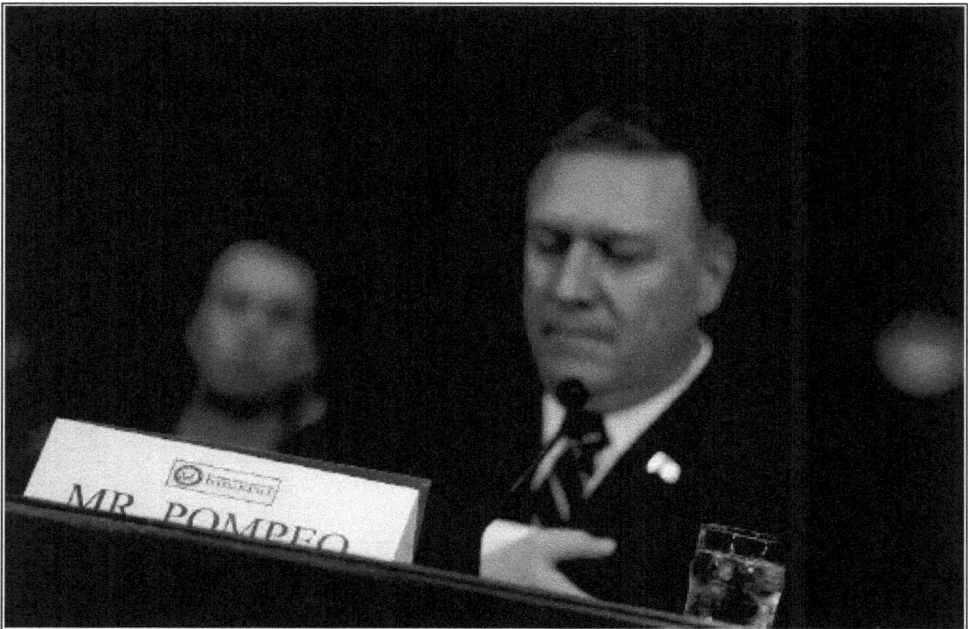

CARLOS BARRIA / REUTERS

Mike Pompeo testifies before a Senate Intelligence hearing on his nomination to become director of the CIA, Washington, January 2017.

Policymakers should be able to aggressively question analytic judgments and raw reporting without being accused of politicizing intelligence. Politicization can occur only when intelligence professionals alter their findings to meet policymakers' desires. Aggressive questioning should be welcomed, in fact, because it forces analysts to defend their reasoning and leads to deeper understanding of the raw reporting that underlies their judgments. Policymakers need to understand not only what the intelligence community knows but also what it doesn't know. Having learned from the mistakes made about Iraq, the intelligence community now carefully conveys the level of confidence it places on the judgments it makes. Policymakers should also ask what could cause these judgments to change, what are the truly critical factors on which each judgment rests—"linchpin analysis," in intelligence speak.

Policymakers sometimes go too far and try to intimidate analysts into changing or shading their judgments to fit a political objective. When that doesn't work, some have gone so far as to set up their own intelligence shops, as Secretary of Defense Donald Rumsfeld and Deputy Secretary of Defense Paul Wolfowitz did in establishing the Office of Special Plans at the Pentagon in the run-up to the Iraq war to find politically desired linkages between Saddam Hussein and al Qaeda. But policymakers cannot politicize intelligence professionals who refuse to go along.

RISKY BUSINESS

To gain an edge over their targets, intelligence officers have to take risks. They must face unimaginable dangers and overcome incredible obstacles just to collect small but critical fragments of an unknown story. The essential national service they provide should not be dismissed, minimized, or overlooked by the president or senior policymakers. Law enforcement officers, first responders, and members of the military and intelligence services are the only Americans who voluntarily agree to run mortal risks for their fellow citizens. The CIA's memorial wall honors 117 officers who died in the line of duty; many of them still remain undercover. As George Tenet, the former director of central intelligence, has said, their families and colleagues must have "the courage to bear great grief in silence." Their service and that of currently serving officers should be respected.

Policymakers cannot politicize intelligence professionals who refuse to go along.

When using intelligence, policymakers need to be risk takers of a different kind. They might base a decision on intelligence that turns out to be wrong. A presidentially approved covert operation may be blown, leading to death, embarrassment, or retaliation. A foreign leader may learn that U.S. intelligence has been monitoring his or her phone calls. Skiers, when renting equipment, sign a waiver that begins with the phrase, "Skiing is an inherently dangerous sport." National security policymakers should mentally sign a similar waiver—and in practice ask themselves, "How much risk are we willing to take?"

Faced with the complexities of international crises, presidents are often drawn to the option of covert action. As Henry Kissinger once described it, "We need an intelligence community that, in certain complicated situations, can defend the American national interest in the gray areas where military operations are not suitable and diplomacy cannot operate." Covert action can range from propaganda to coup plotting to paramilitary operations. Used judiciously, it can be an effective foreign policy tool, but it cannot substitute for not having a policy in the first place.

Covert actions pose three risks for policymakers: exposure, failure, and the blowback of unintended consequences. Traditionally, covert action was the mandate solely of the CIA, with operations requiring a finding personally signed by the president and timely notification of Congress. In recent years, under the guise of force protection or battlefield preparation, the U.S. military has conducted intelligence activities abroad that would have required a covert-action finding if conducted by the CIA. New policymakers with appropriate clearances will need to fully understand the extent of this activity and the potential risks engendered by it.

Both policymakers and the intelligence community are accountable to the American people, yet ensuring such accountability can be difficult. The public understands that the intelligence community must keep secrets, but that very secrecy can fuel concerns about government overreach. These days, it is not always clear where a foreign threat ends and a domestic threat begins, and government agencies need to share intelligence in order to prevent disasters. However, given the power and reach of U.S. capabilities for intercepting communications, such sharing raises legitimate concerns about civil liberties and privacy.

A healthy conversation and debate on these issues are both necessary and wise. The intelligence community does not ignore such concerns, but often, it wants to address the tension between collection and protection in classified venues such as the Foreign Intelligence Surveillance Court, the National Security Council, or the congressional intelligence oversight committees. But those concerned with civil liberties want them addressed in the public domain. However the balance is achieved, the American people must be confident that the internal controls are appropriate and that external oversight has sufficient visibility to be effective.

FORWARD GUIDANCE

To meet current and future challenges, the U.S. intelligence community must constantly innovate and improve. A new administration can bring a fresh perspective on how best to organize and modernize the community, and positive change should be embraced and welcomed by intelligence professionals. The new national security team, however, needs to balance a desire for change against the potential disruption drastic change may cause in the intelligence mission. Although disruption can be a positive force in technology and business, in the intelligence community, it could carry serious risks.

Future relations between intelligence producers and consumers in Washington remain uncertain. The gravity of the presidency and the weight of the decisions the president alone must make almost inevitably change the person who sits behind the desk. As the complexities of the international challenges facing the United States become clear, the value of intelligence in dealing with those challenges may lead senior administration officials to rely more heavily on the intelligence community. Mike Pompeo, the director of the CIA; Gina Haspel, the deputy director; and Dan Coats, the director of national intelligence, are well positioned to lead the community into the future. But the importance of the intelligence community's relationship with the president himself cannot be overstated. If human sources don't believe that their intelligence will make a difference, they may not take the extra chance to meet with a case officer. If friendly foreign intelligence services believe that their most sensitive information might be leaked to the public as part of political score-settling, they will hold back and be disinclined to share. Leaders of the intelligence community must be able to walk into the president's office at any time and be received openly and professionally.

The members of the U.S. intelligence community serve their country proudly and help it remain strong. Their professionalism is a bulwark of American democracy, and they should be respected for the work they do. Unless quickly rectified, policymakers' misconceptions about intelligence professionals and their motivations could endanger U.S. national security. The relationship needs to be recalibrated, with policymakers gaining a deeper understanding of and appreciation for the work of intelligence professionals—a mission in which "alternative facts" have no place.

JAMI MISCIK is CEO of Kissinger Associates and former Deputy Director for Intelligence at the CIA. She is also Chair of *Foreign Affairs'* Advisory Board.

Where to Go From Here

Rebooting American Foreign Policy

Richard N. Haass

I'll have what Xi's having: Xi and Trump at Mar-a-Lago, Florida, April 2017.

Every new U.S. administration takes several months to staff itself properly, master new and often unfamiliar responsibilities, and develop a comprehensive strategy for American foreign policy. The Trump administration's start has been especially rocky. But the administration has already executed a noticeable course shift on foreign policy and international affairs, exchanging some of its early outsider rhetoric and personnel for more conventional choices. If it can continue to elaborate and professionalize its new approach, it could achieve a number of successes. But for that to happen, the administration will have to act with considerably greater discipline and work to frame its policies toward regional and global issues as part of a coherent, strategic approach to international relations that benefits the United States, its allies and partners, and the world at large.

THE CHALLENGE IN ASIA

President Donald Trump has properly concluded that the greatest threat to U.S. national security is North Korea's accelerating nuclear and missile programs, which may give Pyongyang the ability to launch nuclear-tipped missiles at the continental United States in a matter of months or at most years. The president also seems to have concluded, correctly, that several decades of U.S. policy, mostly consisting of sanctions and on-again, off-again negotiations aimed at ridding North Korea of nuclear weapons, have failed. The challenge now is to choose among the three plausible alternative options for moving forward: acceptance, military intervention, or more creative diplomacy. A fourth possibility, that of regime change, does not qualify as a serious option, since it is impossible to assess its chances or consequences.

In theory, the United States and other powers could accept a North Korean nuclear capability and rely on deterrence to lower the risk of an attack and missile defenses to reduce the damage should one occur. The problem is that deterrence and defenses might not work perfectly—so the acceptance option means living with a perpetual risk of catastrophe. Moreover, even if Pyongyang were deterred from using the weapons it developed, it would still be able to transfer them to other actors for the right price. And even if its nuclear capability were never used or transferred, acquiescence to North Korea's continued possession of nuclear weapons would further dilute the nonproliferation regime and conceivably lead Japan and South Korea to rethink their nonnuclear postures.

North Korean leader Kim Jong Un watching a military drill, March 2016.

Military intervention could be either preventive (moving deliberately to destroy a gathering threat) or preemptive (moving quickly to head off an immediate one). The problem here is that any such strike would be a huge leap into the unknown with possibly devastating consequences. Officials could not know in advance just what a military operation would accomplish and how the North Koreans would react. Given Pyongyang's ability to destroy large parts of Seoul using conventional, nonnuclear forces, the South Korean government is understandably leery of the intervention option, and so any moves along these lines would need to be planned and coordinated with extreme care.

The unattractiveness of both acceptance and intervention is what keeps bringing policymakers back to the third option, trying to cap and reverse the North Korean nuclear threat through negotiations. But as decades of failed efforts have proved, diplomacy is no panacea. So the challenge on this front is not just getting back to the table but also figuring out how to make rapid progress once there. This could be done by breaking the issue's resolution into two stages, with an interim deal that would freeze Pyongyang's nuclear and missile programs, followed by longer-term efforts to reduce and eliminate the programs entirely.

The interim deal could best be executed as a bilateral agreement between the United States and North Korea, with other governments kept involved and informed through consultations. The negotiations should have a deadline for reaching agreement, to ensure that Pyongyang doesn't use the talks simply to buy time for further progress on its weapons programs. The North would have to agree to pause its testing of warheads and missiles while the negotiations continued, and the United States and South Korea would have to agree not to strike North Korea during the same period. In exchange for accepting a comprehensive, open-ended freeze on its nuclear and missile programs, intrusive inspections designed to ensure that the freeze was being honored, and a ban on any transfers of nuclear materials or missile technology to third parties, North Korea would get some sanctions relief and an agreement formally ending the Korean War, a form of de facto recognition. Follow-on talks would deal with denuclearization and other concerns (such as human rights) in exchange for an end to the sanctions and the normalization of ties.

An interim agreement would not solve the North Korean nuclear problem, but it would keep it from getting any worse and lower the risks of war and instability—as positive a result as one could imagine in the current circumstances. Since Chinese pressure on North Korea would be essential to achieve such a deal, this option would build logically on the administration's early investment in good relations with its counterpart in Beijing. And even if diplomacy failed again, at least the United States would have demonstrated that it tried negotiations before turning to one of the other, more controversial options.

Over time, "America First" will lead others to put themselves first.

As for the U.S. relationship with China itself, the administration's primary goal should be to emphasize cooperation over North Korea, the most urgent item on the national security agenda. The two countries' economic integration gives both Washington and Beijing a stake in keeping relations on course. China's leaders are likely to focus for the foreseeable future on domestic concerns more than foreign policy ones, and the United States should let them do so. That means leaving in place long-standing U.S. policies on bilateral issues such as Taiwan, trade, arms sales, and the South China Sea; the Trump administration should avoid adopting positions on these issues that could either trigger a distracting crisis or compromise U.S. interests. The result would be a "North Korea first," but not a "North Korea only," U.S. policy toward China.

Regarding the Asia-Pacific more generally, the administration should reassure U.S. allies about the United States' continued commitment to the region—something that has been called into question by Trump's abrupt withdrawal from the Trans-Pacific Partnership and by various statements from the president and other administration officials. It would have made more sense for Washington to work with the other signatories to amend the TPP (as it appears to be doing in regard to the North American Free Trade Agreement) and join the modified pact. This remains an option, although it may be difficult to achieve. Failing that, the administration could attempt to work out an understanding with Congress that would allow the United States to join the TPP but commit the country to certain courses of punitive action in specific circumstances (currency manipulation, intellectual property theft, large government subsidies, and so on), similar to what was done when it came to U.S.-Soviet arms control agreements. The understanding would be codified and voted on at the same time as the trade agreement itself, as a binding package, to reassure the agreement's critics.

FRIENDS AND FOES

In Europe, Washington should pursue stability. The EU is imperfect in many ways, but it remains a source of peace and prosperity on the continent. Its continued erosion or breakup would represent a major setback not just for crucial U.S. allies but also for the United States itself, both strategically and materially. The EU's next few years will already be tense thanks to the negotiations over Brexit and possible crises in Italy and elsewhere. The United States has little leverage to bring to bear on the continent's immediate future, but at the very least, Washington should voice its support for the EU and stop signaling its sympathy for its opponents.

Russia has been aggressively supporting just such anti-EU forces in order to weaken and divide what it sees as a hostile foreign actor, and Russia's interference in Western elections needs to be thoroughly investigated and aggressively countered. Washington's challenge will be figuring out how to support Europe and NATO and check Russia's political skullduggery while remaining open to cooperation with Moscow on making at least parts of Syria safe for residents, on counterterrorism, and on other issues of mutual concern. The administration has made its point that NATO members ought to spend more on defense; going forward, it would be more useful to discuss how to get more defensive bang for the bucks being spent. And although there is no case for bringing Ukraine into NATO, there is one for doing more to support its self-defense. Consistent with this, the sanctions against Russia levied over its actions in Ukraine should continue until those actions stop or, in the case of Crimea, are reversed.

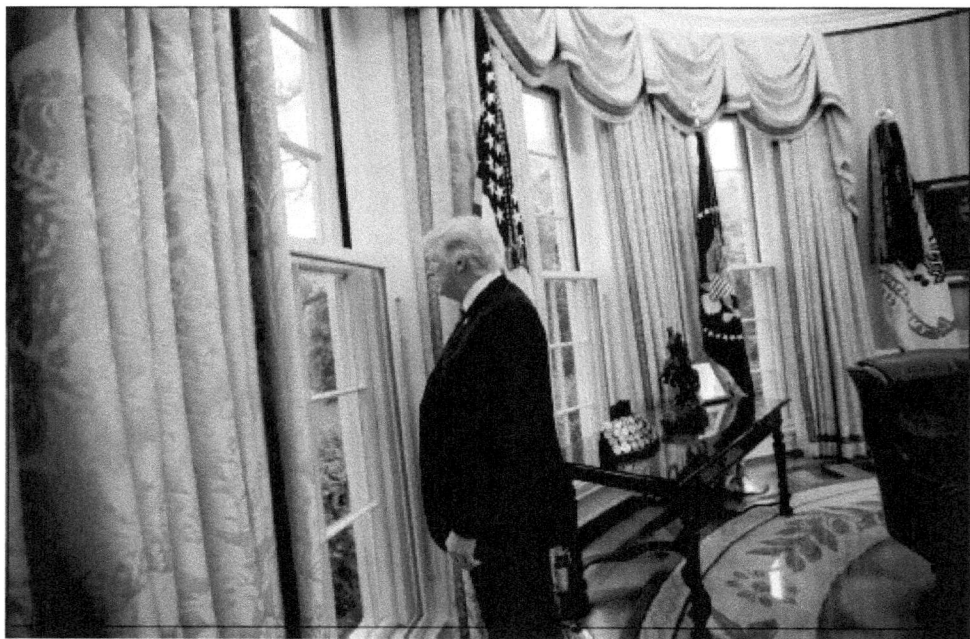

Carlos Barria / REUTERS

Trump in the Oval Office, April 2017.

In the Middle East, the Trump administration helped itself significantly with its quick, limited air strike in April in response to the Syrian government's use of chemical weapons. The strike reinforced the international norm against the use of weapons of mass destruction and sent a reassuring signal to local partners, who, during the Obama years, had become increasingly worried about Washington's willingness to back up its threats with actions. The challenge now is to embed such actions in a broader strategy toward the Syrian conflict and the Middle East at large.

However desirable a change of regime in Syria may be, it is unlikely to come from within anytime soon, and it would be incredibly difficult and costly to accomplish from without. Nor is the United States well positioned to ensure that a successor regime will be more desirable. For the foreseeable future, therefore, Washington should concentrate its attention on attacking the Islamic State, or ISIS, and weakening the group's hold on territory in Iraq and Syria. The Iraqi army is capable enough to control liberated areas in Iraq, but there is no counterpart to it yet in Syria, so getting such a force ready, drawn primarily from local Sunni groups, should be a priority.

Turkey is a U.S. ally, but it can no longer be considered a true partner. Under Recep Tayyip Erdogan's increasingly authoritarian rule, the chief goal of Turkish foreign policy seems to be the suppression of Kurdish nationalism, even at the price of undermining the anti-ISIS effort. Washington correctly chose to increase its armed support for Syrian Kurds fighting ISIS—and because this will cause friction with Ankara, it should reduce U.S. dependence on access to Turkish military bases for these and other operations.

The Iran nuclear deal is imperfect, but the administration has been right not to tear it up and start over. Doing so would leave Washington isolated and Tehran unconstrained. What the United States should do instead is insist on full compliance with the agreement's terms, counter Iran's regional push for influence where it can, and prepare for how to constrain Iran's nuclear might after the deal expires. At the same time, Washington should resist being drawn in too deeply on the side of Saudi Arabia and the United Arab Emirates in Yemen. The conflict there is fast becoming a military disaster and a humanitarian tragedy, and the fact that the rebels are backed by Iran is insufficient justification for getting trapped in a quagmire.

The struggle against terrorism will be long, difficult, and never fully successful.

The Trump administration has said various things about its intentions regarding what used to be called "the Middle East peace process." The unfortunate fact is that neither the Israelis nor the Palestinians appear ready to move forward; the most Washington can achieve right now may be to keep the situation from deteriorating further (which is actually very important, because in the Middle East, things can always get worse). There is no reason to believe that the situation is ripe for resolution or ambitious diplomatic efforts. The administration should concentrate instead on reducing the odds of violence around Jerusalem's holy sites (something that argues against moving the U.S. embassy to Jerusalem), strengthening the hand of Palestinian moderates, limiting settlement activity, and exploring unilateral but coordinated arrangements that would improve on the status quo and set the stage for more ambitious diplomacy should the parties decide they are prepared to make meaningful compromises for peace.

The Middle East is not the place to look for quick or easy victories. The struggle against terrorism, jihadist and otherwise, will inevitably be long, difficult, and never fully successful. Terrorism cannot be eliminated, only combated, and such an effort will continue to require a mix of intelligence sharing and cooperation with friendly governments, persistent pressure on terrorist financing and recruitment, and occasional military action. The number of U.S. forces deployed in Iraq, Syria, and the region more generally will likely need to be maintained or selectively increased.

A TIME TO LEAD

Back during the George W. Bush administration, in trying to articulate what the United States really wanted from China, Robert Zoellick, the deputy secretary of state, framed the question as one of whether Beijing was prepared to act as "a responsible stakeholder" in the international system. The concept is a useful one and applies now to the United States, the founder and dominant power within that system. So what constitutes responsible behavior for Washington in the world at large at this juncture?

One element is giving appropriate attention to both interests and ideals. The Trump administration has shown a clear preference for not involving the United States in the internal affairs of other countries. Such realism is often warranted, given Washington's multiple priorities and limited leverage in such matters. But there is a danger in taking this approach too far, since prudent nonintervention can all too easily shade into active support for deeply problematic regimes. Careless relationships with "friendly tyrants," as such rulers used to be called, have burned the United States often in the past, and so it is worrying to see Washington take what look like the first steps down such a path again with Egypt, the Philippines, and Turkey. Friends need to speak candidly to friends about the errors they may be making. Such communications should normally take place privately and without sanction. But they do need to occur, lest the United States tarnish its reputation, encourage even worse behavior, and set back efforts to promote more open societies and stability around the world. The president should also understand that what he says about U.S. institutions, including the media, the judiciary, and Congress, is listened to closely around the world and has the potential to reduce respect for the United States while encouraging leaders elsewhere to weaken the checks and balances on their rule.

Aleppo, Syria, March 2015.

Another element of responsible behavior is continued support for international aid and development, which is a cost-effective way to promote American values and interests simultaneously. In recent memory, for example, Colombia was racked by civil war and served as a major source of drugs coming into the United States. Since then, the provision of hundreds of millions of dollars in U.S. aid has helped stabilize the country and secure a delicate peace—saving countless lives and dollars as a result. Similar stories play out when Washington helps foreign partners address terrorism, piracy, drug trafficking, poverty, deforestation, and epidemic disease. When it gives aid wisely and conditionally, the United States is not a soft touch but a smart investor.

The administration would do well to tone down some of its rhetoric on trade. Technological innovation has been a much more important source of domestic job losses than trade or offshoring, and embracing protectionism will only encourage others to do the same, in the process killing off more jobs. What is needed is a full-fledged national initiative to increase economic security, consisting of educational and training programs, temporary wage support for displaced workers, the repatriation of corporate profits to encourage investment at home, and infrastructure spending. The last, in particular, is a multipurpose tool that could at once create jobs, increase competitiveness, and build the country's resilience against natural disasters and terrorism.

Something similar holds for immigration, which should be treated as a practical more than a political issue. However the American body politic ultimately decides to handle legal and illegal immigration policy, the danger to the country supposedly posed by immigrants and refugees has been exaggerated and is not a major national security threat. The administration should cease gratuitously insulting its southern neighbor (and promoting anti-Americanism there) by insisting that Mexico pay for a border wall. And singling out individuals from Muslim countries for special scrutiny and differential treatment risks radicalizing significant numbers of their coreligionists at home and abroad.

The administration (and Congress) needs to be careful not to set the country on a path of rapidly increasing debt. The danger is that a combination of steep corporate and individual tax cuts, higher levels of defense spending and higher interest rates, and no reform of entitlements will do just that. Financing the debt will come to crowd out other useful forms of spending and investment (reducing American competitiveness) and leave the United States more vulnerable to market forces and the politically motivated decisions of governments that are large holders and purchasers of U.S. Treasuries.

Russia's interference in Western elections needs to be thoroughly investigated and aggressively countered.

One last policy matter involves the climate. The intensity of the opposition in some quarters to the 2015 Paris accord and to acceptance of climate change as the result of human activity is something of a mystery. The agreement is a model of creative multilateralism, one totally consistent with sovereignty; the administration would be wise to embrace it. The targets set for U.S. greenhouse gas emissions are goals the United States set for itself; as a result, the government retains the right to change them, when and how it sees fit. The good news is that the availability of new technologies, state and local regulations, and the requirements for access to many global markets will likely mean that the United States can meet its Paris goals without sacrificing economic growth.

As for personnel and process, the administration hurt itself at first by underestimating the complexity of running the government and taking a petulant and idiosyncratic approach to appointments. As a result, most senior national security and foreign policy staff positions are being filled on a temporary basis by civil servants or have been left open entirely, hamstringing effective government operations. Any thoughts of a major bureaucratic restructuring should be postponed until the administration is filled with the requisite number of qualified officials.

Trump clearly prefers an informal decision-making process, with various voices included and many points of entry, and presidents get their way. But such an approach has downsides as well as upsides, and if the administration wants to avoid the dangers that come with excessive improvisation, it needs to ensure that the formal National Security Council policy process dominates the informal one—and that significant informal deliberations are ultimately integrated into the formal process rather than carried on separately.

The president also clearly prefers to be unpredictable. This can make sense as a tactic, but not as a strategy. Keeping foes off balance can be useful, but keeping friends and allies off balance is less so—especially friends and allies that have put their security in American hands for generations. The less steady they judge those hands to be, the more they may decide to look out for themselves, ignoring Washington's requests and considering side deals to protect their interests. Frequent policy reversals, even those that are welcome, come at a substantial cost to the United States' credibility and to its reputation for reliability.

Down that route lies the unraveling of the postwar order that the United States has worked so hard to create and maintain. It is important not to forget that the United States has been remarkably well served by this order. Where things have gone the most wrong—in Korea, when U.S. forces marched north of the 38th parallel in what would become a costly and unsuccessful effort to reunify the peninsula by force, in Vietnam, in Iraq—it was because of overreach by U.S. policymakers rather than a requirement to act on behalf of the order.

But that order is now in decline. Many of its components need to be modernized or supplemented, and new rules and arrangements are needed to deal with the various challenges of globalization. But the international project should be a renovation, not a teardown. New challenges may have arisen, but the old challenges have not gone away, so the old solutions to them are still necessary even if they are no longer sufficient. The strategic focus for U.S. foreign policy should be preservation and adaptation, not disruption, so that the United States and those willing to work with it can better contend with the regional and, even more, the global challenges that increasingly define this era.

The EU is imperfect in many ways, but it remains a source of peace and prosperity on the continent.

In that regard, the president's campaign slogan of "America First" was and is unfortunate, because it appears to signal a narrower U.S. foreign policy, one lacking in a larger purpose or vision. It has been interpreted abroad as suggesting that friends and allies now come second, at best. Over time, "America First" will lead others to put themselves first, which in turn will make them less likely to take into account (much less give priority to) American interests and preferences.

The slogan also unfortunately reinforces the mistaken notion that there is a sharp tradeoff between money and effort spent on international affairs and those spent on domestic concerns. In a global world, Americans will inevitably be affected by what happens beyond their country's borders. The United States needs both guns and butter, and national security is determined by how well a country meets its external and internal challenges alike. The good news is that the United States, which now spends only half the percentage of its wealth on defense that it did during the Cold War, can afford both.

If the administration does decide to retain the phrase, it should at least recognize its shortcomings and counteract them. This means finding ways to make clear that although the United States does follow its own interests, it does not do so at its friends' and partners' expense. American patriotism can be defined and operationalized in ways compatible with responsible global leadership. And figuring out how to do that from here on in is the Trump administration's central challenge.

RICHARD N. HAASS is President of the Council on Foreign Relations and the author of *A World in Disarray: American Foreign Policy and the Crisis of the Old Order.*

© Foreign Affairs

The Korean Missile Crisis

Why Deterrence Is Still the Best Option

Scott D. Sagan

Kim Jong Un waves during a celebration of the founding of the ruling Workers' Party of Korea in Pyongyang, October 2015.

It is time for the U.S. government to admit that it has failed to prevent North Korea from acquiring nuclear weapons and intercontinental ballistic missiles that can reach the United States. North Korea no longer poses a nonproliferation problem; it poses a nuclear deterrence problem. The gravest danger now is that North Korea, South Korea, and the United States will stumble into a catastrophic war that none of them wants.

The world has traveled down this perilous path before. In 1950, the Truman administration contemplated a preventive strike to keep the Soviet Union from acquiring nuclear weapons but decided that the resulting conflict would resemble World War II in scope and that containment and deterrence were better options. In the 1960s, the Kennedy administration feared that Chinese leader Mao Zedong was mentally unstable and proposed a joint strike against the nascent Chinese nuclear program to the Soviets. (Moscow rejected the idea.) Ultimately, the United States learned to live with a nuclear Russia and a nuclear China. It can now learn to live with a nuclear North Korea.

Doing so will not be risk free, however. Accidents, misperceptions, and volatile leaders could all too easily cause disaster. The Cold War offers important lessons in how to reduce these risks by practicing containment and deterrence wisely. But officials in the Pentagon and the White House face a new and unprecedented challenge: they must deter North Korean leader Kim Jong Un while also preventing U.S. President Donald Trump from bumbling into war. U.S. military leaders should make plain to their political superiors and the American public that any U.S. first strike on North Korea would result in a devastating loss of American and South Korean lives. And civilian leaders must convince Kim that the United States will not attempt to overthrow his regime unless he begins a war. If the U.S. civilian and military leaderships perform these tasks well, the same approach that prevented nuclear catastrophe during the Cold War can deter Pyongyang until the day that communist North Korea, like the Soviet Union before it, collapses under its own weight.

DANGER OF DEATH

The international relations scholar Robert Litwak has described the current standoff with North Korea as "the Cuban missile crisis in slow motion," and several pundits, politicians, and academics have repeated that analogy. But the current Korean missile crisis is even more dangerous than the Cuban one. For one thing, the Cuban missile crisis did not involve a new country becoming a nuclear power. In 1962, the Soviet Union was covertly stationing missiles and nuclear warheads in Cuba when U.S. intelligence discovered the operation. During the resulting crisis, Cuban Prime Minister Fidel Castro feared an imminent U.S. air strike and invasion and wrote to Soviet Premier Nikita Khrushchev advocating a nuclear strike on the United States "to eliminate such danger forever through an act of clear legitimate defense, however harsh and terrible the solution would be." When Khrushchev received the message, he told a meeting of his senior leadership, "This is insane; Fidel wants to drag us into the grave with him!" Luckily, the Soviet Union maintained control of its nuclear weapons, and Castro did not possess any of his own; his itchy fingers were not on the nuclear trigger.

Kim, in contrast, already presides over an arsenal that U.S. intelligence agencies believe contains as many as 60 nuclear warheads. Some uncertainty still exists about whether North Korea can successfully mount those weapons on a missile capable of hitting the continental United States, but history cautions against wishful thinking. The window of opportunity for a successful U.S. attack to stop the North Korean nuclear program has closed.

At the time of the Cuban missile crisis, both the American and the Soviet nuclear war plans were heavily geared toward preemption. Each country's system featured a built-in option to launch nuclear weapons if officials believed that an enemy attack was imminent and unavoidable. This produced a danger that the strategist Thomas Schelling called "the reciprocal fear of surprise attack." That fear was why Khrushchev was so alarmed when a U.S. U-2 spy plane accidentally flew into Soviet airspace during the crisis. As he wrote to U.S. President John F. Kennedy on the final day of the crisis: "Is it not a fact that an intruding American plane could be easily taken for a nuclear bomber, which might push us to a fateful step?" Today, the world faces an even more complex and dangerous problem: a three-way fear of surprise attack. North Korea, South Korea, and the United States are all poised to launch preemptive strikes. In such an unstable situation, the risk that an accident, a false warning, or a misperceived military exercise could lead to a war is alarmingly high.

The same approach that prevented nuclear catastrophe during the Cold War can deter Pyongyang.

Another factor that makes today's situation more dangerous than the Cuban missile crisis is the leaders involved. In 1962, the standoff included one volatile leader, Castro, who held radical misperceptions of the consequences of a nuclear war and surrounded himself with yes men. Today, there are two such unpredictable and ill-informed leaders: Kim and Trump. Both men are rational and ruthless. Yet both are also prone to lash out impulsively at perceived enemies, a tendency that can lead to reckless rhetoric and behavior.

This danger is compounded because their senior advisers are in a poor position to speak truth to power. Kim clearly tolerates no dissent; he has reportedly executed family members and rivals for offering insufficiently enthusiastic praise. For his part, Trump often ignores, ridicules, or fires those who disagree with him. In May, The New York Times reported that Trump had described his national security adviser, Lieutenant General H. R. McMaster, as "a pain" for subtly correcting him when he made inaccurate points in meetings. And in June, the spectacle of U.S. department secretaries falling over themselves to declare their deep devotion to Trump and flatter him on live television during the administration's first full cabinet meeting brought to mind the dysfunctional decision-making in dictatorships. Any leader who disdains expertise and demands submission and total loyalty from his advisers, whether in a democracy or in a dictatorship, will not receive candid assessments of alternative courses of action during a crisis.

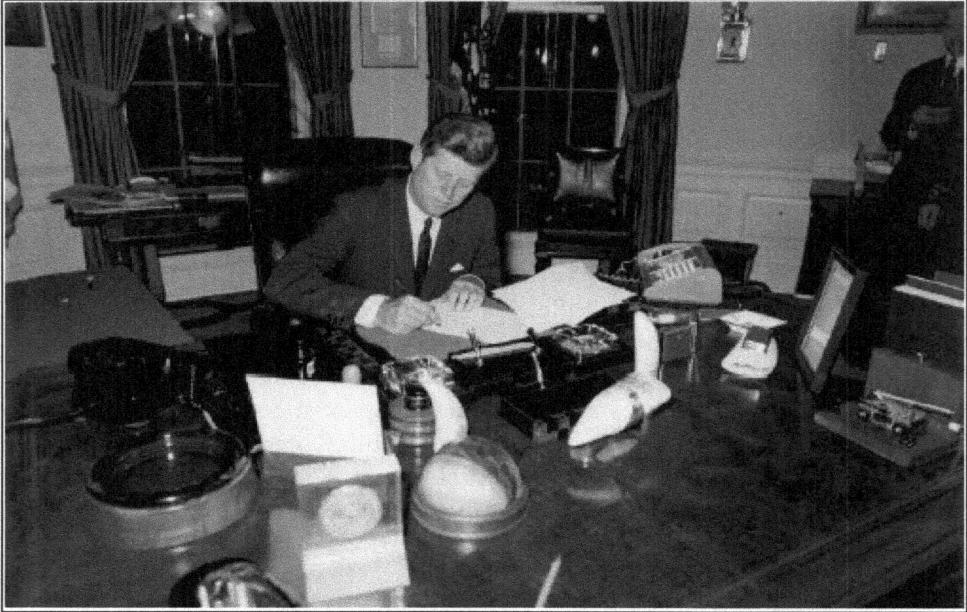

President John F. Kennedy signs a proclamation for the interdiction of the delivery of offensive weapons to Cuba during the Cuban missile crisis, October 1962.

TONE-DEFCON

Trump's poor decision-making process highlights another disturbing contrast with the Cuban missile crisis. In 1962, strong civilian leaders countered the U.S. military's dangerously hawkish instincts. When the Joint Chiefs of Staff recommended an immediate air strike and an invasion of Cuba, Kennedy insisted on the more prudent option of a naval blockade. Together with his subsequent refusal to retaliate with an air strike after an American U-2 spy plane was shot down over Cuba, Kennedy's approach reflected the best kind of cautious crisis management.

Now, however, it is the senior political leadership in the United States that has made reckless threats, and it has fallen to Secretary of Defense James Mattis (a former general) and senior military officers to serve as the voices of prudence. In early August, Trump warned: "North Korea best not make any more threats to the United States. They will be met with fire and fury like the world has never seen." By appearing to commit to using nuclear force in response to North Korean threats, he broke sharply with U.S. deterrence policy, which had previously warned of military responses only to acts of aggression. Vice President Mike Pence, Secretary of State Rex Tillerson, and UN Ambassador Nikki Haley have not echoed Trump's "fire and fury" rhetoric, but they have repeated the worrying mantra that "all options are on the table."

That phrase may sound less threatening than Trump's comments, but it still leaves itself open to misinterpretation. To some listeners, it just suggests that Washington is considering limited military options. But from a North Korean perspective, the statement implies that the United States is contemplating launching a nuclear first strike. This would not be an altogether unreasonable conclusion for Pyongyang to draw. In 2008, U.S. President George W. Bush stated that all options were on the table when it came to U.S. tensions with Iran, and when a reporter explicitly asked Bush whether that included "nuclear options," Bush simply repeated himself: "All options are on the table." The Obama administration made a commitment, in its 2009 Nuclear Posture Review, not to use nuclear weapons against any non-nuclearweapons state that was in compliance with its nonproliferation commitments. But then Secretary of Defense Robert Gates quickly added that "because North Korea and Iran are not in compliance with the Nuclear Nonproliferation Treaty, for them, all bets are off. All options are on the table."

Such rhetoric is dangerous. The U.S. government must convince Kim that an attack on the United States or its allies would spell the end of his regime. But it is equally important that U.S. leaders acknowledge loudly and often that it would be a disaster for the United States to start a war. If those in the White House do not do so, the civilian and military leadership in the Pentagon should more forcefully and publicly make this point.

To back this rhetoric up, the United States should take some military options off the table, starting with a preventive nuclear war. A preemptive strike, the use of force when a country considers an adversary's first strike imminent and unavoidable, can sometimes be justified strategically and legally as "anticipatory self-defense." But preventive war—starting a war to prevent another country from taking future action or acquiring a dangerous capability—is rarely justified and arguably contrary to the UN Charter.

U.S. military officers are trained to follow orders from political authorities, unless they are clearly unconstitutional. The Constitution, however, says nothing about what to do if a president's orders are legal but also crazy. This leads to bizarre situations, such as the response that Admiral Scott Swift, the commander of the U.S. Pacific Fleet, gave when he was asked at a seminar at the Australian National University in July if he would launch a nuclear strike against China "next week" if Trump ordered him to do so. The admiral should have said that the hypothetical scenario was ridiculous and left it at that. Instead, he answered, "Yes."

The current Korean missile crisis is even more dangerous than the Cuban one.

Trump's volatility has produced a hidden crisis in U.S. civil-military relations. In 1974, during the final days of Richard Nixon's presidency, when Nixon had become morose and possibly unstable, Secretary of Defense James Schlesinger told the chairman of the Joint Chiefs of Staff, General George Brown, that if Nixon gave military orders, Brown should contact Schlesinger before carrying them out. Schlesinger's action was extraconstitutional but nonetheless wise, given the extraordinary circumstances. The U.S. government faces similar dangers every day under Trump. Mattis and senior military leaders should be prepared to ignore belligerent tweets, push back against imprudent policies, and resist any orders that they believe reflect impetuous or irrational decision-making by the president. Their oath, after all, is not to an individual president; it is to "support and defend the Constitution of the United States." The Constitution's 25th Amendment lays out procedures on how to relieve an impaired president of his responsibilities. If senior military leaders believe at any time that Trump is impaired, they have a duty to contact Mattis, who should then call for an emergency cabinet meeting to determine whether Trump is "unable to discharge the powers and duties of his office" and thus whether to invoke the 25th Amendment.

WHAT YOU DON'T KNOW CAN HURT YOU

One similarity with the Cuban missile crisis is that those Americans who think the United States should attack North Korea exaggerate the prospects that U.S. military action would succeed and underestimate the costs of a war. In 1962, the CIA and the military assumed that there were no nuclear weapons in Cuba and, on that basis, recommended air strikes and an invasion. But the intelligence assessment was wrong. Well over 60 nuclear warheads, gravity bombs, and tactical nuclear weapons had already arrived in Cuba, and one missile regiment was already operational by the time the Joint Chiefs were advising military action. Any attack on Cuba would almost certainly have led to nuclear strikes on the United States and against invading U.S. forces.

Today, U.S. intelligence finds itself once again in the dark. It does not know the status of North Korea's warheads or the locations of its missiles. For example, when the North Koreans successfully tested an intercontinental ballistic missile in late July, it came as a complete surprise to the United States and demonstrated that North Korea can now build such missiles, store them, take them out of storage, and launch them, all before the United States could react. Yet U.S. military leaders have failed to pour cold water on the idea of a U.S. first strike. Instead, they have added fuel to the fire.

Consider the complaint expressed by General Joseph Dunford, the chairman of the Joint Chiefs of Staff, at the Aspen Security Forum in July that "many people have talked about the military options with words such as 'unimaginable.'" Dunford insisted that, to the contrary, "it is not unimaginable to have military options to respond to North Korean nuclear capability. What's unimaginable to me is allowing a capability that would allow a nuclear weapon to land in Denver, Colorado…. And so my job will be to develop military options to make sure that doesn't happen." Dunford should have reinforced deterrence. Instead, he created a redline that Kim may have already crossed.

The military's job is to come up with options. That involves thinking the unthinkable. But it is also military leaders' responsibility to offer brutal honesty to political leaders and the public. When it comes to the current conflict with North Korea, that means admitting that there are no military options that do not risk starting the most destructive war since 1945.

kim Hong-Ji / REUTERS

South Korean marines during a U.S.-South Korean exerices, Pohang, South Korea, April 2017.

WHY THERE'S NO MILITARY SOLUTION

Some Trump supporters, including former UN Ambassador John Bolton and Trump's evangelical adviser Robert Jeffress, have argued that a U.S. strike to assassinate Kim is the best solution. Any attempt to "decapitate" the regime, however, would be a gamble of epic proportions. The history of unsuccessful U.S. decapitation attempts, including those launched against the Libyan leader Muammar al-Qaddafi in 1986 and the Iraqi leader Saddam Hussein in 1991 and again in 2003, warns against such thinking. Moreover, Kim may well have ordered his generals to launch all available weapons of mass destruction at the enemy if he is killed in a first strike—as did Saddam before the 1990–91 Gulf War. There is no reason to think that the North Korean military would fail to carry out such an order.

U.S. leaders should also resist the temptation to hope that limited, or "surgical," conventional attacks on North Korean missile test sites or storage facilities would end the nuclear

threat. Proponents of this course believe that the threat of further escalation by the United States would deter North Korea from responding militarily to a limited first strike. But as the political scientist Barry Posen has explained, this argument is logically inconsistent: Kim cannot be both so irrational that he cannot be deterred in general and so rational that he could be deterred after having been attacked by the United States. Moreover, even a limited attack by the United States would appear to North Korea as the beginning of an invasion. And because no first strike could destroy every North Korean missile and nuclear weapon, the United States and its allies would always face the prospect of nuclear retaliation.

Mattis and senior military leaders should be prepared to resist any orders that they believe reflect impetuous or irrational decision-making by the president.

Nor can missile defense systems solve the problem. The United States should continue to develop and deploy missile defenses because they complicate North Korean military planning, and any missiles that Pyongyang aims at U.S. or allied military targets are missiles not aimed at American, Japanese, or South Korean cities. But military leaders should be candid about the limits of U.S. ballistic missile defenses. Most such systems have failed numerous tests, and even the most effective ones, such as the Terminal High Altitude Area Defense, or THAAD, system, could be overwhelmed if North Korea fired multiple missiles—even dummy missiles—in a salvo at one target. That is why North Korea has been practicing launching several missiles simultaneously. Any prudent U.S. planner should therefore assume that in the event of an attack, some North Korean nuclear-armed missiles would reach their targets. Even in the best-case scenario, in which only a few North Korean nuclear weapons penetrated U.S. defenses, the consequences would prove catastrophic.

Estimating the potential fatalities in a limited nuclear strike is difficult, but the nuclear weapons scholar Alex Wellerstein has designed a useful modeling tool called NUKEMAP, which uses data from the Hiroshima and Nagasaki bombings to provide rough estimates of how many people would die in a nuclear strike. After North Korea conducted its sixth nuclear test, in early September, Japanese, South Korean, and U.S. intelligence agencies reportedly provided a range of estimates of the weapon's explosive yield, with an average estimate of around 100 kilotons. According to NUKEMAP, a single 100-kiloton nuclear weapon detonated above the port city of Busan, in South Korea (which was shown as a target in a recent North Korean press release), would kill 440,000 people in seconds. A weapon of that size detonated over Seoul would kill 362,000; over San Francisco, the number would be 323,000. These estimates, moreover, include only immediate blast fatalities, not the deaths from fires after a nuclear detonation or the longer-term deaths that would result from radioactive fallout. Those secondary effects could easily cause the number of dead to double.

Even if a war were limited to the Korean Peninsula, the costs would still be unacceptable. According to a detailed study published in 2012 by the Nautilus Institute, a think tank based in California, North Korea has thousands of conventional artillery pieces along the demilitarized zone that by themselves could inflict some 64,000 fatalities in Seoul on the first day of a war. A major attack on South Korea could also kill many of the roughly 154,000 American civilians and 28,000 U.S. service members living there. If the North Korean regime used its large arsenal of chemical and biological weapons, the fatalities would be even higher. Finally, there are a number of nuclear power plants near Busan that could be damaged, spreading radioactive materials, in an attack. All told, one million people could die on the first day of a second Korean war.

KCNA

A military drill in North Korea, March 2016.

ACCIDENTAL WAR

Even if the United States forswore preventive conventional or nuclear strikes, the danger of an accidental war caused by the mutual fear of a surprise attack would remain. South Korea increasingly (and quite openly) relies on a strategy of preemption and decapitation. In 2013, General Jeong Seungjo, the chairman of the South Korean Joint Chiefs of Staff, announced that "if there is a clear intent that North Korea is about to use a nuclear weapon, we will eliminate it first even at the risk of a war," adding that "a preemptive attack against the North trying to use nuclear weapons does not require consultation with the United States and it is the right of self-defense." A white paper published by the South Korean Ministry of National Defense in 2016 featured an illustration of several missiles being fired at and a group of South Korean commandos attacking the "war command" building in Pyongyang. (Unsurprisingly, the North Koreans have similar ideas about preemption: in April 2016, in response to U.S. and South Korean military exercises, North Korean state media reported that "the revolutionary armed forces of [North Korea] decided to take preemptive attack as the mode of its military counteraction.... The right to nuclear preemptive attack is by no means the U.S. monopoly.")

Reducing the risk of war will require an end to U.S. threats of first-strike regime change.

In such a tense environment, one government's preemptive-war plan can look a lot like a first-strike plan to its enemies. Would Seoul see the movement of Pyongyang's nuclear missiles out of the caves in which they are stored as a drill, a defensive precaution, or the start of an attack? Would Pyongyang mistake a joint U.S.–South Korean exercise simulating a decapitation attack for the real thing? Could an ill-timed inflammatory tweet by Trump provoke a military response from Kim? What if a radar technician accidentally put a training tape of a missile launch into a radar warning system—which actually happened, creating a brief moment of panic, during the Cuban missile crisis? Add in the possibility of an American or a South Korean military aircraft accidentally entering North Korean airspace, or a North Korean nuclear weapon accidentally detonating during transport, and the situation resembles less a Cuban missile crisis in slow motion than an August 1914 crisis at the speed of Twitter.

The fear of a U.S. attack explains why Kim believes he needs a nuclear arsenal. Pyongyang's nuclear weapons development undoubtedly appeals to Kim's domestic audience's desire for self-sufficiency. But that is not its primary purpose. Kim's spokespeople have stressed that he will not suffer the fate of Saddam or Qaddafi, both of whom gave up their nuclear programs only to be attacked later by the United States. The North Korean nuclear arsenal is not a bargaining chip. It is a potent deterrent designed to prevent a U.S. attack or disrupt one that does occur by destroying U.S. air bases and ports through preemption, if possible, but in retaliation if necessary. And if all else fails, it is a means for exacting revenge by destroying Kim's enemies' cities. That may sound implausible, but keep in mind that Castro recommended just such an attack in 1962.

KEEP CALM AND DETER ON

Living with a nuclear North Korea does not, in Dr. Strangelove's terms, mean learning "to stop worrying and love the bomb." On the contrary, it means constantly worrying and addressing every risk. U.S. policy should aim to convince Kim that starting a war would lead to an unmitigated disaster for North Korea, especially as his own ministers and military advisers may be too frightened of his wrath to make that argument themselves. The United States should state clearly and calmly that any attack by North Korea would lead to the swift and violent end of the Kim regime.

Kim may be under the illusion that if North Korea were to destroy U.S. air bases and kill hundreds of thousands of Americans, Japanese, and South Koreans, the American public would seek peace. In fact, it would likely demand vengeance and an end to Kim's regime, regardless of the costs. Such a war would be bloody, but there is no doubt which side would prevail. There are few, if any, military targets in North Korea that the United States could not destroy with advanced conventional weapons in a long war. And the Kim regime cannot ignore the possibility of U.S. nuclear retaliation.

The more difficult challenge will be convincing Kim that the United States will not attack him first. Reducing the risk of war will therefore require an end to U.S. threats of first-strike regime change. In August, Tillerson told reporters that the United States did not seek to overthrow Kim unless he were to begin a war. Other American leaders should consistently echo Tillerson's comments. Unfortunately, the Trump administration's rhetoric has been anything but consistent.

Should the United States succeed in bringing North Korea back to the negotiating table, it should be prepared to offer changes to U.S. and South Korean military exercises in exchange for limits on—and notifications of—North Korean missile tests and the restoration of the hotline between North and South Korea. The United States should also continue to extend its nuclear umbrella to South Korea to reduce the incentive for Seoul to acquire its own nuclear arsenal. Some have argued for a return of U.S. tactical nuclear weapons to air bases in South Korea, but such weapons would be vulnerable to a North Korean first strike. A better option would be to keep nuclear capable bombers at Guam on ground alert. Or the United States could borrow a tactic it used in the wake of the Cuban missile crisis. To assuage Moscow, Washington promised to remove its Jupiter ballistic missiles from Turkey after the crisis. But to reassure Ankara, it also assigned some submarine-based missiles to cover the same retaliatory targets in the Soviet Union that the Jupiter missiles had and arranged for a U.S. submarine to visit a Turkish port. Today, occasional U.S. submarine calls at South Korean harbors could enhance deterrence without provoking North Korea.

In 1947, the American diplomat George Kennan outlined a strategy for the "patient but firm and vigilant containment" of the Soviet Union. Writing in this magazine, he predicted that such a policy would eventually lead to "either the breakup or the gradual mellowing of Soviet power." He was right. In the same way, the United States has deterred North Korea from invading South Korea or attacking Japan for over 60 years. Despite all the bluster and tension today, there is no reason why Kennan's strategy of containment and deterrence cannot continue to work on North Korea, as it did on the Soviet Union. The United States must wait with patience and vigilance until the Kim regime collapses under the weight of its own economic and political weakness.

SCOTT D. SAGAN is Caroline S. G. Munro Professor of Political Science and a Senior Fellow at the Center for International Security and Cooperation at Stanford University.

When Stalin Faced Hitler

Who Fooled Whom?

Stephen Kotkin

JOHANNES HÄHLE

German troops cross the Soviet border, 22 June 1941.

Through the first four decades of his life, Joseph Stalin achieved little. He was born in 1878 to a poor family in Gori, Georgia, then part of the Russian empire. His father was a cobbler; his mother, a cleaning lady and seamstress. Stalin's childhood, illnesses and mishaps included, was largely normal for the time. He received good marks in school and, as a teenager, got his poems published in well-regarded Georgian periodicals. ("To this day his beautiful, sonorous lyrics echo in my ears," one reader would later recall.) But he did not sit for his final-year exams at the Tiflis Seminary and failed to graduate. Instead of becoming a priest, he became an underground revolutionary fighting tsarist oppression, spending the next 20 years hiding, organizing, and serving time in prison and internal exile in Siberia.

Stalin's life was altered forever by the outbreak of total war in 1914, which helped precipitate the Russian tsar's abdication in February 1917 and, later that year, a putsch by radical leftists led by Vladimir Lenin. Suddenly, the 39-year-old Stalin was a leading member of the new Bolshevik regime.

He played a central role in the Russian Civil War and the creation of the Soviet Union. In 1922, Lenin appointed him head of the Communist Party. A month later, Lenin was incapacitated by a stroke, and Stalin seized his chance to create his own personal dictatorship inside the larger Bolshevik one. Beginning in the late 1920s, he forced through the building of a socialist state, herding 120 million peasants onto collective farms or into the gulag and arresting and murdering immense numbers of loyal people in the officer corps, the secret police, embassies, spy networks, scientific and artistic circles, and party organizations.

The vast shadow of Stalin the despot often hides Stalin the human being. He collected watches. He played skittles and billiards. He loved gardening and Russian steam baths. He liked colored pencils—blue, red, and green. He drank mineral water and wines from his native Georgia. He smoked a pipe, using tobacco from cigarettes, which he would unroll and slide into the pipe—usually two cigarettes' worth—and then light with matches. He kept his desk in order.

Stalin had a passion for books, which he marked up and filled with placeholders to find particular passages. His personal library would ultimately grow to more than 20,000 volumes. He annotated works by Karl Marx and Lenin, of course, but also Russian translations of Plato and Clausewitz, as well as the writings of Alexander Svechin, a former tsarist officer whom Stalin never trusted but who demonstrated that the only constant in war was an absence of constants. Among Russian authors, Stalin's favorite was probably Anton Chekhov, who portrayed villains, and not just heroes, with complexity. Still, judging by the references scattered among his writings and speeches, he spent more time reading Soviet-era literature. His jottings in whatever he read were often irreverent: "Rubbish," "fool," "scumbag," "piss off," "ha-ha!"

Stalin in 1932.

Stalin's manners were coarse, and his sense of humor perverse. But he cultivated a statesmanlike appearance, editing out his jokes and foul language from the transcripts of official gatherings. He appears to have had few mistresses, and definitely no harem. His family life was neither particularly happy nor unhappy. Personal life was subsumed in politics.

Stalin spoke softly, sometimes inaudibly, because of a defect in his vocal cords. He relished being called Koba, after the Georgian folk-hero avenger (and a real-life benefactor who had underwritten Stalin's education). But one childhood chum had called him Geza, a Gori-dialect term for the unusual gait Stalin had developed after an accident. He had to swing his hip all the way around to walk. A childhood bout with smallpox had left lifelong scars on his nose, lower lip, chin, and cheeks.

It is tempting to find in such deformities the wellsprings of bloody tyranny: torment, self-loathing, inner rage, bluster, a mania for adulation. His pockmarks were airbrushed out of public photographs, and his awkward stride was hidden from public view. (Film of him walking was prohibited.) But people who met him saw the facial disfigurement and odd movement; they also discovered that he had a limp handshake and was not as tall as he appeared in photographs. He stood five feet seven inches, roughly the same as Napoleon and one inch shorter than Adolf Hitler. And yet, despite their initial shock on seeing him for the first time—could this be Stalin?—most people found that they could not take their gaze off him, especially his expressive eyes.

THE DREAM PALACE

Stalin saw himself and his country as menaced from every direction. After seizing power in 1917, Lenin and his followers had obsessed over the "capitalist encirclement" their coup had brought about: now, this structural paranoia fed, and was fed by, Stalin's personal paranoia. Such were the paradoxes of power: the closer the country got to achieving socialism, Stalin argued, the sharper the class struggle became; the more power Stalin personally wielded, the more he still needed. Triumph shadowed by treachery became the dynamic of both the revolution and his life. Beginning in 1929, as the might of the Soviet state and Stalin's personal dictatorship grew and grew, so, too, did the stakes. His drive to build socialism would prove both successful and shattering, and deeply reinforcing of his hypersuspicious, vindictive disposition.

Communism was an idea, a dream palace whose attraction derived from its seeming fusion of science and utopia, and Stalin was an ideologue. In the Marxist conception, capitalism had created great wealth by replacing feudalism, but then promoted only the interests of the exploiter class, at the expense of the rest of humanity. Once capitalism was overcome, the thinking went, the forces of production would be unleashed as never before. Exploitation, colonization, and imperialist war would give way to solidarity, emancipation, and peace. To be sure, socialism in practice had been difficult to imagine. But whatever it was, it could not be capitalism. Logically, socialism would be built by eradicating private property, the market, and "bourgeois" parliaments and putting in their place collective property, socialist planning, and people's power. Of course, as Stalin and many other Marxists avowed, the capitalists would never allow themselves to be buried. Rather, they would fight to the death against socialism, using every means—lies, espionage, murder—because this was a war in which only one class could emerge victorious. Socialism, therefore, would also have to use mass violence and deceit. The most terrible crimes became morally imperative acts in the name of creating paradise on earth.

The purported science of Marxism-Leninism ostensibly explained why the world had so many problems (class) and how it could be made better (class warfare), with a role for all. People's otherwise insignificant lives became linked to building an entirely new world. To collect grain or operate a lathe was to strike a hammer blow at world imperialism. It did not hurt that those who took part stood to gain personally: idealism and opportunism are always reinforcing.

Accumulated resentments, too, fueled the aspiration to become significant. People under the age of 29 made up nearly half of the Soviet population, giving the country one of the youngest demographic profiles in the world, and the youth proved especially attracted to a vision that put them at the center of a struggle to build tomorrow today.

Stalin personified communism's lofty vision. A cult would be built around him, singling him out as vozhd, an ancient Slavic word that came to mean something like "supreme leader"—the Russian equivalent of "duce" or "führer." Stalin resisted the cult, calling himself "shit compared with Lenin." According to his close associate Anastas Mikoyan, Stalin once rebuked another Soviet official, saying, "Why do you praise me alone, as if one man decides everything?" Whether Stalin's objections reflected false modesty or genuine embarrassment remains hard to say, but he indulged the prolonged ovations he received in public. "At first," recalled Vyacheslav Molotov, who served as Stalin's principal lieutenant for decades, "he resisted the cult of personality, but then he came to like it a bit."

Stalin was a ruler of seemingly irreconcilable contradictions. He could flash burning anger; he could glow with a soft, capacious smile. He could be solicitous and charming; he latched on to perceived slights and compulsively sought revenge. He prided himself on his voracious reading and his ability to quote the wisdom of Marx or Lenin; he resented fancy-pants intellectuals who he thought put on airs. He possessed a phenomenal memory and a mind of scope; his intellectual horizons were severely circumscribed by primitive theories of class struggle and imperialism. He developed a feel for the aspirations of the masses and incipient elites; he almost never visited factories or farms, or even state agencies, instead reading about the country he ruled in secret reports and newspapers. He was a cynic about everyone's supposed base motives; he lived and breathed his own ideals.

Stalin did what winning leaders do: he articulated and drove toward a consistent goal, in his case a powerful state backed by a unified society that had eradicated capitalism and built industrial socialism. "Murderous" and "mendacious" do not begin to describe him. At the same time, Stalin galvanized millions. His colossal authority was rooted in a dedicated party, a formidable governing apparatus, and Marxist-Leninist ideology. But his power was magnified many times over by ordinary people, who projected onto him their ambitions for social justice, peace, abundance, and national greatness. Dictators who amass great power often retreat into pet pursuits, expounding interminably on their obsessions and paralyzing the state. But Stalin's obsession was a socialist great power, and he labored day and night to build one. Stalin was a myth, but he proved equal to the myth.

"A TREMENDOUS CHAP"

Hitler was 11 years Stalin's junior, born in 1889 in a frontier region of Austria-Hungary. He lost his father at age 13 and his mother at 18. (The Jewish physician who tended to his mother would recall that in 40 years of practicing medicine, he had never seen anyone as broken with grief over a mother's death as Hitler.) At age 20, Hitler found himself on a bread line in Vienna, his inheritance and savings nearly spent. He had twice been rejected from Vienna's Academy of Fine Arts ("sample drawing unsatisfactory") and was staying in a homeless shelter behind a railway station. A vagrant on the next bed recalled that Hitler's "clothes were being cleaned of lice, since for days he had been wandering about without a roof and in a terribly neglected condition." Soon, with a small loan from an aunt, Hitler got himself into a group home for men. He managed to find odd jobs, such as painting picture postcards and drafting advertisements. He also frequented the city's public libraries, where he read political tracts, newspapers, the philosopher Arthur Schopenhauer, and the fiction of Karl May, set in the cowboys-and-Indians days of the American West or in the exotic Near East.

Hitler dodged the Austrian draft. When the authorities finally caught up with him, they judged the undernourished and gloomy youth unfit for service. He fled across the border to Munich, and in August 1914, he joined the German army as a private. He ended World War I still a private, but the war's aftermath transformed his life. He would be among the many who migrated from the political left to the right in the chaotic wake of imperial Germany's defeat.

Under Stalin, the most terrible crimes became morally imperative acts in the name of creating paradise on earth.

Film footage from 1918 shows Hitler marching in the funeral procession of provincial Bavaria's murdered leader, a Jewish Social Democrat; he is wearing two armbands, one black (for mourning) and the other red. In April 1919, after Social Democrats and anarchists formed the Bavarian Soviet Republic, the Communists quickly seized power; Hitler, who contemplated joining the Social Democrats, served as a delegate from his battalion's soviet (council). He had no profession to speak of but appears to have taken part in leftist indoctrination of the troops. Ten days before Hitler's 30th birthday, the Bavarian Soviet Republic was quickly crushed by the so-called Freikorps, made up largely of war veterans. Hitler remained in the military because a superior, the chief of the German army's "information" department, had the idea of sending him to an antileftist instructional course and then using him to infiltrate leftist groups. The officer recalled that Hitler "was like a tired stray dog looking for a master" and "ready to throw in his lot with anyone who would show him kindness." The assignment as an informant led to Hitler's involvement in a minuscule right-wing group, the German Workers' Party, which had been established to draw workers away from communism and which Hitler, with the assistance of rabidly anti-Semitic émigrés from the former imperial Russia, would remake into the National Socialist German Workers' Party, or Nazi Party.

Although he had begun to earn a reputation as a transfixing far-right agitator, Hitler remained a marginal figure. When Stalin was the new general secretary of the

Communist Party of the largest state in the world, Hitler was in prison for a failed 1923 attempt to seize power in Munich, which would be derided as "the Beer Hall Putsch." He was convicted and sentenced to five years. Still, he managed to turn his trial into a triumph. One of the judges remarked, "What a tremendous chap, this Hitler!" Indeed, even though Hitler was an Austrian citizen, the presiding judge allowed him to stay in Germany, reasoning that the law requiring deportation "cannot apply to a man who thinks and feels as German as Hitler, who voluntarily served for four and a half years in the German army at war, who attained high military honors through outstanding bravery in the face of the enemy, was wounded."

During his first two weeks in prison, Hitler refused to eat, believing he deserved to die, but letters arrived congratulating him as a national hero. Richard Wagner's daughter-in-law, Winifred, sent paper and pencil, encouraging him to write a book. Hitler had an attendant in confinement, Rudolf Hess, who typed his dictation, creating an autobiography dedicated to the 16 Nazis killed in the failed putsch. In Mein Kampf, Hitler portrayed himself as a man of destiny and pledged to revive Germany as a great power and rid it of Jews, anointing himself "the destroyer of Marxism." In December 1924, after serving only 13 months, he was released. But his book sales disappointed, a second book failed to find a publisher, and his Nazi Party struggled at the ballot box. Lord D'Abernon, the British ambassador to Berlin at the time, summarized Hitler's political life after his early release from prison as "fading into oblivion."

History is full of surprises. That this Austrian member of a fringe political movement would become the dictator of Germany, and Stalin's principal nemesis, was scarcely imaginable in 1924. But Hitler turned out to be a master improviser: often uncertain, but a man possessed of radical ideas who sensed where he was ultimately going and grasped opportunities that came his way. Stalin, too, was a strategist in that sense: a man of radical ideas able to perceive and seize opportunities that he did not always create but turned to his advantage. The richest opportunities perceived by Stalin and Hitler were often supposedly urgent "threats" that they inflated or invented. History is driven by the interaction of geopolitics, institutions, and ideas—but it takes historical agents to set it all in motion.

Stalin's direct experience of Germany consisted of just a few months in 1907 in Berlin, where he stopped on the way back to Russia from a Bolshevik meeting in London. He studied but never mastered the German language. But like several tsarist predecessors, Stalin was a Germanophile, admiring that country's industry and science—in a word, its modernity. But for the longest time, Stalin had no idea of Hitler's existence.

Then, in 1933, Hitler was handed the wheel of the great state Stalin admired. The lives of the two dictators had run in parallel, as the historian Alan Bullock wrote. But it was the intersection that would matter: two very different men from the peripheries of their societies who were bloodily reviving and remaking their countries, all while unknowingly (and then knowingly) drawing ever closer. It was not only the German people who turned out to be waiting for Hitler.

Hitler addresses the Reichstag, Berlin, March 1933.

FACE-OFF

On Saturday, June 21, 1941, Stalin paced and paced in his Kremlin office, with his usual short steps, gripping a pipe. Inside the triangular Kremlin, the Imperial Senate formed its own triangular stronghold, and Stalin's wing was a fortress within the fortress. Even the regime personnel with regular Kremlin passes needed a special pass to enter Stalin's wing. It came to be known to regime insiders as the Little Corner. The walls in the offices were lined with shoulder-height wood paneling, under the theory that wood vapors enhanced air quality, and the elevators were paneled with mahogany. Behind Stalin's working desk hung a portrait of Lenin. In a corner, on a small table, stood a display case with Lenin's death mask. Another small table held several telephones. ("Stalin," he would answer.) Next to the desk was a stand with a vase holding fresh fruit. In the rear was a door that led to a room for relaxation (although rarely used for that purpose), with oversize hanging maps and a giant globe. In the main office, between two of the three large windows that let in afternoon sun, sat a black leather couch where, in his better moods, Stalin sipped tea with lemon.

Over the years, people who were granted an audience with him surmised that he paced to control his explosive emotions or, alternatively, to unnerve those in his company. Invariably, he would be the only one in the room standing, trundling back and forth, sidling up to people while they were speaking. Only a few intimates knew that Stalin suffered nearly constant pain in the joints of his legs, which may have been a genetic condition and which movement partly alleviated. He also strolled the Kremlin grounds, usually alone, touching the leaves on the trees and shooing away black ravens. (Afterward, guards would come and massacre the birds.)

Stalin had eliminated private property and made himself responsible for the Soviet equivalents of Washington, Wall Street, and Hollywood all rolled into one, and all rolled into one person. He complained of fatigue, especially toward the end of his long workdays, and suffered from insomnia, a condition never acknowledged publicly. A tiny group of insiders knew of his infections and multiday fevers. Rumors of various health problems had circulated abroad, and the use of foreign doctors had long ago been discontinued. But a narrow circle of Russian physicians had acquired detailed knowledge of his illnesses and of his bodily deformities, including his barely usable left arm, the thick, discolored toenails on his right foot, and the two webbed toes on his left foot (an omen, in traditional Russian folklore, of Satanic influence). For long periods, Stalin resisted being seen by any doctor, and he had ceased using medicines from the Kremlin pharmacy that were issued in his name. The household staff had stopped bringing his meals from the Kremlin canteen, cooking them in his apartment instead and, in his presence, tasting from the plates. All the same, Stalin's stomach was a wreck. He suffered from regular bouts of diarrhea.

Hitler was a master improviser who grasped opportunities that came his way.

The Imperial Senate had been built by the Teutonic empress of Russia, Catherine the Great, for "the glorification of Russian statehood." A few decades after its opening, in the early fall of 1812, Napoleon had arrived with his invading forces. Members of the French Grande Armée—which included many Protestants and Catholics from Germany, Italy, and Poland—had defecated in the Kremlin's Orthodox churches and taken potshots at the holy icons. After cunning Russian resistance starved the occupiers, a retreating Napoleon had ordered the Kremlin blown to pieces. Heavy rains limited the damage, but the explosives destroyed parts of the walls and several towers. The Imperial Senate suffered a fire.

The long, red-carpeted corridors around the Little Corner were attended by an army of sentries. "See how many of them there are?" Stalin once remarked to a military commander. "Each time I take this corridor, I think, which one? If this one, he will shoot me in the back, and if it is the one around the corner, he will shoot me in the front." The commander was dumbfounded by such paranoia: after all, there had never been a single genuine assassination attempt against Stalin. But the "Man of Steel"—"deeper than the ocean, higher than the Himalayas, brighter than the sun, teacher of the universe," in the words of the Kazakh national poet—was being stalked from afar.

In the summer of 1941, it seemed clear that Hitler had won World War II. He had annexed his native Austria, the Czech lands, much of Poland, and a strip of Lithuania, creating the Greater Germany that in 1871 Otto von Bismarck had deliberately avoided forging during the wars of German unification (deeming Austria-Hungary's existence vital for the balance of power). Hitler's troops had occupied the Balkans, Denmark, the Low Countries, Norway, and northern France. Leaders loyal to the führer ruled Bulgaria, Croatia, Finland, Hungary, Italy, Romania, and Spain. Hitler essentially controlled all of Europe from the English Channel to the Soviet border; only Sweden and Switzerland remained neutral, and both were cooperating with Nazi Germany economically. True, the defiant British still refused to come to terms, but London could never overturn Berlin's continental dominance.

Stalin was strictly observing the nonaggression pact that Germany and the Soviet Union had signed in August 1939. At that time, Hitler, who had decided to swallow Poland by force, needed to keep the Soviet Union out of a possible anti-German coalition with France and the United Kingdom. Stalin extracted a highly favorable bargain. As Hitler rampaged across the rest of Europe, Stalin avoided having to face Germany's military might and, taking advantage of the situation, occupied and soon annexed the Baltic states, eastern Poland, and the eastern European regions of Bukovina and Bessarabia. Moreover, in exchange for Soviet grain and oil, Stalin received advanced machine tools and state-of-the-art weaponry from Germany.

Stalin's apprenticeship in high-stakes diplomacy had shown him to be cunning but also opportunistic, avaricious, obdurate. His approach had remained the same: prepare for war with a massive armaments buildup, yet do everything to avoid fighting while allowing the British and the Germans to go at each other. This had worked, until Germany—aided by the cornucopia of Soviet raw materials—conquered France in the summer of 1940, and Germany was freed up to turn its troops toward the Soviet Union. The two geopolitical and ideological rivals, as a result of their shared aggrandizement, had acquired a common border.

Molotov in 1945.

Now, after half a year of contradictory secret reports about a possible German invasion of the Soviet Union, intelligence warnings of an imminent titanic war were coming from everywhere. In Moscow, German embassy personnel were evacuating, taking with them oil paintings, antique rugs, and silver. The Soviet secret police reported that the Italian embassy, too, had received instructions to evacuate. Earlier in the day, a Soviet agent in Bulgaria had reported that a German emissary had said that "a military confrontation is expected on June 21 or 22." The Chinese Communist leader Zhou Enlai reported to officials at the Comintern, the international communist organization, that his nationalist rival, Chiang Kai-shek, "is declaring insistently that Germany will attack the USSR, and is even giving a date: June 21, 1941!" This prompted the head of the Comintern to call Molotov. "The situation is unclear," Molotov told him. "There is a major game under way. Not everything depends on us."

FAKE NEWS

It was a hot, stifling day, and Stalin's top aide, Alexander Poskryobyshev, was sweating profusely, his window open but the leaves on the trees outside utterly still. The son of a cobbler, like the despot he served, Poskryobyshev occupied the immediate outer office through which all visitors had to pass, and invariably they would spray him with questions—"Why did the Master have me summoned?" "What's his mood?"—to which he would laconically answer, "You'll find out." He was indispensable, handling all the phone calls and document piles in just the way the despot preferred. But Stalin had allowed Lavrenti Beria, the feared head of the secret police, to imprison Poskryobyshev's beloved wife as a "Trotskyite" in 1939. (Beria had sent a large basket of fruit to their two girls; he then executed their mother.)

Poskryobyshev sat at his desk trying to cool down with a bottle of mineral water. On Stalin's instructions, at around 2:00 PM, he phoned General Ivan Tyulenev, head of the Moscow Military District. Soon the general heard Stalin's muffled voice asking, "Comrade Tyulenev, what is the situation concerning Moscow's antiaircraft defenses?" After a brief report, Stalin said, "Listen, the situation is unsettled and therefore you should bring the antiaircraft defenses of Moscow up to 75 percent of their readiness state."

Poskryobyshev placed the latest intelligence, delivered by a field courier, on Stalin's desk. Almost all of it was hearsay, rather than purloined documents. The reports were contradictory, contaminated with obviously false information, and often delivered with skepticism. In London, the Soviet ambassador to the United Kingdom wrote in his report that he considered a German attack "unlikely" despite having received information to the contrary from British intercepts of secret German military communications. In Berlin, however, the Soviet ambassador to Germany, after months of equivocation, finally averred that Germany's actions signaled an imminent invasion. But Stalin evidently concluded that his envoy in Berlin had been fed disinformation and remarked that he was "not such a smart fellow."

Stalin labeled as "disinformation" whatever he chose not to believe.

For Stalin, the question was not whether war with the Nazi regime was inescapable but whether it was inescapable this year. Scores and scores of invasion warnings had accumulated on his desk, but 14 specific dates that intelligence reports had identified as the day when Germany would attack had come and gone. The only remaining possibilities were "June 22–25" and "June 21 or 22." The invasion window would soon shut, because of the short time remaining until the onset of winter. Stalin was virtually home free for another year. Of course, warnings of impending war were even splashed across the front pages of newspapers all over the world. But knowing how he himself made use of the press, Stalin took the screaming headlines to be planted provocations. He reasoned that the Americans and the British wanted nothing more than for the Germans and the Soviets to become embroiled in war. He was right, of course. But as a result, he dismissed all warnings of a German attack. He knew that Germany was experiencing severe shortages and reasoned that it needed even more supplies from him, thus a German invasion would be self-defeating because it would put those supplies at risk. He knew further that Germany had lost World War I because it had fought on two fronts, and so he reasoned that the Germans understood that it would be suicidal for them to attack the Soviet Union in the east before defeating the United Kingdom in the west.

This kind of reasoning had become a trap for Stalin, allowing him to conclude that the colossal buildup of German forces on his doorstep was not a sign of imminent attack but rather Hitler attempting to blackmail him into giving up territory and making other concessions without a fight. Indeed, a brilliant Nazi disinformation campaign fed the Soviet global spy network with incessant reports about German demands that would follow the vast eastern military buildup. Thus, even Stalin's best intelligence said both that war was coming and that there would be blackmail. And if the latter were true, the former need not be.

When Stalin damned his intelligence as contaminated by disinformation, therefore, he was right. But the despot had no idea which parts were disinformation and which might be accurate intelligence. He labeled as "disinformation" whatever he chose not to believe.

READY OR NOT, HERE I COME

Colonel Georgy Zakharov, a decorated fighter pilot, had been ordered to conduct a full daylight reconnaissance of the border region on the German side, and he reported that the Wehrmacht was poised to invade. The NKGB, the Soviet secret police agency, had discovered that German saboteurs brazenly crossing the border had been instructed that "in the event German troops cross the frontier before they return to Germany, they must report to any German troop unit located on Soviet territory."

Soviet counterintelligence noted vigorous German recruitment of disaffected people in the Baltic region, Belarus, and Ukraine, who were forming underground groups and engaging in terrorism long after Stalin's supposed annihilation of the perceived fifth column during the Great Terror. Overburdened Soviet rail lines that were needed to transport troops westward were swamped with tens of thousands of "anti-Soviet elements" being deported. German tanks, warplanes, and pontoons had been advanced into an inner zone protected by barbed wire; now the wire was being removed. The click and whir of German motors resounded across to the Soviet side of the frontier.

At the centerpiece of the Little Corner, a felt-covered conference table, Stalin had held countless sessions devoted to war preparations. He had forced into being upward of 9,000 new industrial enterprises during three Five-Year Plans, and Soviet military production grew even faster than GDP for a decade. He had overseen the formation of 125 new divisions just since 1939, and the Red Army now stood at 5.37 million troops, the largest military force in the world. It had 25,000 tanks and 18,000 fighter planes, three to four times the size of Germany's stocks. Stalin knew that Germany was underestimating this massive force out of prejudice as well as ignorance, so he had arranged German visits to Soviet aviation and tank factories, and even allowed German planes nearly unimpeded reconnaissance of Soviet troop concentrations, airfields, naval bases, and fuel and ammunition depots. Stalin also had his spies spread rumors that, if attacked, Soviet aircraft would assault Berlin with chemical and biological agents. In Hitler's shoes, Stalin would have been deterred.

Stalin clung to his belief that Germany could not attack Russia before defeating the United Kingdom.

Of course, if his own country really was so well armed, why not let an enemy foolishly underestimate it? Because the so-called Winter War between the Soviet Union and Finland, waged in 1939–40, had exposed Soviet military weaknesses not just to Hitler but also to Stalin. (The Soviets had won a crushing victory in the end, but only after being stymied for months by stout Finnish resistance.) The Red Army was still in the middle of a protracted post-Finland technological upgrade and reorganization. The Soviets possessed only around 1,800 advanced heavy tanks; the rest of their tanks were too light relative to their German counterparts. Similarly, the most advanced Soviet warplanes made up just one-quarter of the air force. Stalin's war preparations also bore the mark of his executions of thousands of loyal officers, especially top commanders such as Vasily Blyukher, whose eye had been deposited in his hand before he died under torture in 1938, and the gifted Mikhail Tukhachevsky, whose blood had been splattered all over his "confession" to being a German agent—not long before Stalin concluded the German-Soviet Nonaggression Pact.

Now, 85 percent of the officer corps was 35 or younger; those older than 45 constituted around one percent. Fully 1,013 Soviet generals were under age 55, and only 63 were older than that. Many had been majors just a short time earlier. Out of 659,000 Soviet officers, only around half had completed military school, while one in four had the bare minimum (a few courses), and one in eight had no military education whatsoever.

TONIGHT'S THE NIGHT

Stalin was keenly aware of these realities, and lately, the despot's morose side had gotten the upper hand. "Stalin was unnerved and irritated by persistent reports (oral and written) about the deterioration of relations with Germany," recalled Admiral Nikolai Kuznetsov, the commissar of the Soviet navy, of this period. "He felt that danger was imminent," recalled Nikita Khrushchev, who was at the time the party boss of Ukraine and had spent much of June in Moscow. "Would our country be able to deal with it? Would our army deal with it?"

June 21 happened to be the summer solstice, the longest day of the year—and it must have seemed interminable. At 5:00 PM, Stalin ordered that party secretaries of all Moscow wards were to stay at their posts. At 6:27 PM, Molotov entered the Little Corner—the first visitor, as usual. At 7:05, in walked Beria, Kuznetsov, Georgy Malenkov (a senior Communist Party secretary responsible for cadres), Grigory Safonov (a young deputy procurator general responsible for military courts), Semyon Timoshenko (a senior military commander), Kliment Voroshilov (a deputy head of the government), and Nikolai Voznesensky (the head of state planning). The discussion apparently revolved around recent developments pointing toward war and Stalin's dread of provocations that might incite it.

Stalin's military intelligence estimated that only 120 to 122 of Germany's 285 total divisions were arrayed against the Soviet Union, versus somewhere between 122 and 126 against the United Kingdom (the other 37 to 43 were said to be in reserve). In fact, there were around 200 divisions arrayed against the Soviets—a total of at least three million Wehrmacht soldiers and half a million troops from Germany's Axis partners, as well as 3,600 tanks, 2,700 aircraft, 700,000 field guns and other artillery, 600,000 motor vehicles, and 650,000 horses. The Soviets had massed around 170 divisions (perhaps 2.7 million men) in the west, along with 10,400 tanks and 9,500 aircraft. The two largest armies in world history stood cheek by jowl on a border some 2,000 miles long.

Most conspicuously, German forces had occupied their firing positions; the Soviets had not. To be sure, Stalin had allowed covert strategic redeployments to the western border from the interior. But he would not permit the assumption of combat positions, which he feared would only play into the hands of hawks in the German military who craved war and were scheming to force Hitler's hand. Soviet planes were forbidden from flying within six miles of the border. Timoshenko and Georgy Zhukov, another senior military commander, made sure that frontline commanders did not cause or yield to provocation. Beria also tasked a master assassin with organizing "an experienced strike force to counter any frontier incident that might be used as an excuse to start a war." Soviet commanders could be liquidated by their own side if their forces returned any German fire.

Soviet intelligence was now reporting that not just Germany but also its eastern allies—Finland, Hungary, Romania, and Slovakia—were at full war readiness. But Stalin, having long ago ceded the initiative, was effectively paralyzed. Just about anything he did could be used by Hitler to justify an invasion.

At 7:00 PM, Gerhard Kegel, a Soviet spy in the German embassy in Moscow, had risked his life, slipping out to tell his Soviet handler that German personnel living outside the facility had been ordered to come inside immediately and that "all think that this very night there will be war." At 8:00 PM, a courier arrived to give Stalin, Molotov, and Timoshenko this new piece of intelligence in sealed envelopes. In the Little Corner, Kuznetsov, Safonov, Timoshenko, Voroshilov, and Voznesensky were dismissed at 8:15. Malenkov was dismissed five minutes later. Nothing significant was decided.

Zhukov phoned in to report that yet another German soldier had defected across the frontier and was warning of an invasion within a few hours. This was precisely the kind of "provocation" Stalin feared. He ordered Zhukov to the Kremlin, along with the just-departed Timoshenko. They entered Stalin's office at 8:50. Whereas Molotov and Beria parroted Stalin's denials that Hitler was going to attack, the two peasant-born commanders could see that Germany was coiled to invade. Still, when Stalin insisted otherwise, they presumed that he possessed superior information and insight. In any case, they knew the costs of losing his trust. "Everyone had in their memory the events of recent years," Zhukov would later recall. "And to say out loud that Stalin was wrong, that he is mistaken, to say it plainly, could have meant that without leaving the building, you would be taken to have coffee with Beria."

Nonetheless, the pair evidently used the defector's warnings to urge a general mobilization—tantamount, in Stalin's mind, to war. "Didn't German generals send that defector across the border in order to provoke a conflict?" Stalin asked. "No," answered Timoshenko. "We think the defector is telling the truth." Stalin: "What do we do now?" Timoshenko allowed the silence to persist. Finally, he suggested, "Put the troops on the western border on high alert." He and Zhukov had come prepared with a draft directive.

Stalin had himself tried to engage Hitler even as he waited for the blackmail demands he expected Hitler to issue. "Molotov has asked for permission to visit Berlin, but has been fobbed off," Joseph Goebbels, the Nazi propaganda chief, had written in his diary on June 18. "A naive request."

"The beginning of every war is like opening the door into a dark room," Hitler once said.

Stalin, instead of continuing to wait for an ultimatum from Hitler, could have preempted it. This was the last option he had left, and a potentially powerful one. Hitler feared that the wily Soviet despot would somehow seize the initiative and unilaterally, publicly declare dramatic, far-reaching concessions to Germany. Stalin appears to have discussed possible concessions with Molotov, but if he did, no record survives. Evidently, Stalin expected Germany to demand Ukraine, the Caucasian oil fields, and unimpeded transit for the Wehrmacht through Soviet territory to engage the British in the Near East and India. A cunning despot could have publicly declared his willingness to join the hostilities against the United Kingdom, exacting revenge against the great power he most reviled and, crucially, robbing Hitler of his argument that the British were holding out against Germany in anticipation of eventual Soviet assistance. Instead, or in parallel to that, Stalin could have demonstrably begun the withdrawal of Soviet forces back from the entire frontier, which would have struck at the heart of the Nazi leader's public war rationale: a supposed "preventive attack" against the "Soviet buildup."

Instead of acting cunningly, Stalin clung to his belief that Germany could not attack Russia before defeating the United Kingdom, even though the British did not have an army on the continent and were neither defending territory there nor in a position to invade from there. He assumed that when Hitler finally issued his ultimatum, he would be able to buy time by negotiating: possibly giving in, if the demands were tolerable, and thereby averting war, or, more likely, dragging out any talks beyond the date when Hitler could have launched an invasion, gaining one more critical year, during which the Red Army's technological revamp would advance. Failing that, Stalin further assumed that even if hostilities broke out, the Germans would need at least two more weeks to fully mobilize their main invasion force, allowing him time to mobilize, too. When his spies out of Berlin and elsewhere reported that the Wehrmacht had "completed all war preparations," he did not grasp that this meant that day one would bring full, main-force engagement.

BARBAROSSA BEGINS

In the Little Corner, while the relatively heated discussion with Timoshenko and Zhukov continued, Molotov stepped out. Stalin had him summon the German ambassador, Friedrich Werner von der Schulenburg, to the Imperial Senate for a meeting at 9:30 PM. Schulenburg arrived promptly, direct from overseeing the burning of secret documents at the embassy. The envoy had been deeply disappointed that the Hitler-Stalin Pact, in which he had played an important role, had turned out to be an instrument not for a territorial deal over Poland to avoid war but for the onset of another world war. Now he feared the much-rumored German-Soviet clash, and recently he had gone to Berlin to see Hitler himself and persuade him of Stalin's peaceful intentions but had come back empty-handed. In desperation, Schulenburg had sent his embassy counselor to Berlin to try one last time, but this had failed as well.

Molotov demanded to know why Germany was evacuating personnel, thereby fanning rumors of war. He handed Schulenburg a letter of protest detailing systematic German violations of Soviet airspace and plaintively told him that "the Soviet government is unable to understand the cause of Germany's dissatisfaction in relation to the [Soviet Union], if such dissatisfaction exists." He complained that "there was no reason for the German government to be dissatisfied with Russia." Schulenburg responded that "posing those issues [is] justified," but he shrugged, saying that he was "not able to answer them, because Berlin utterly refrains from informing [me]."

During a state visit to Germany in November 1940, Molotov had gone toe to toe with Hitler in the gargantuan new Reich Chancellery, arguing over clashing spheres of influence in eastern Europe. "No foreign visitor had ever spoken to [Hitler] in this way in my presence," the führer's translator later wrote. But now Molotov could merely express, several times, his regret that Schulenburg was "unable to answer the questions raised."

Molotov shuffled back to Stalin's Little Corner. Suddenly, around 10:00 PM, amid the still suffocating heat, the winds gushed, billowing the curtains at open windows. Then came the thunderclaps. Moscow was struck by a torrential downpour.

Finally, Stalin yielded to his insistent soldiers and accepted their draft directive. Timoshenko and Zhukov rushed out of the Little Corner at 10:20, armed, at long last, with an order for full-scale war mobilization, Directive Number 1. "A surprise attack by the Germans is possible during 22–23 June 1941," it stated. "The task of our forces is to refrain from any kind of provocative action that might result in serious complications." It ordered that "during the night of June 22, 1941, the firing positions of the fortified regions on the state border are to be secretly occupied," that "before dawn on June 22, 1941, all aircraft stationed in the field airdromes are to be dispersed and carefully camouflaged," that "all units are to be put in a state of military preparedness," and that "no further measures are to be carried out without specific instructions." It carried the signatures of Timoshenko and Zhukov. The military men had managed to delete an insertion by the despot that if the Germans attacked, Soviet commanders were to attempt to meet them, to settle any conflict. Still, the document made clear that the military was to prepare for war while doing everything possible to avoid it.

Soviet commanders up and down the frontier were hosting performances, as they generally did on Saturday nights. In Minsk, 150 miles east of the border, the officers' club put on The Wedding at Malinovka, a Soviet comic operetta about a village in the Ukrainian steppes during the civil war. The venue was packed. Attendees included the commander of the critical Western Military District, Dmitry Pavlov; his chief of staff; and his deputies. Six German aircraft had crossed the frontier in Pavlov's region on a recent night. "Never mind. More self-control. I know, it has already been reported! More self-control!" Pavlov was overheard saying on the phone about reports of German actions. As soon as Pavlov put the receiver down and prepared to greet a visitor, the phone rang again. "I know; it has been reported," Pavlov was heard to say. "I know. Those at the top know better than us. That's all." He slammed down the phone. During the operetta, Pavlov was interrupted in his box by a new report of unusual activity: the Germans had removed the barbed wire from their side of the border, and the sound of motors had grown louder, even at a distance. An uninterrupted flow of German mechanized columns was moving forward. Pavlov remained at the show.

Around midnight, the commander of the Kiev Military District called the defense commissariat to report that another German had crossed the border, claiming that Wehrmacht soldiers had taken up their firing positions, with tanks at their start lines. Some 12 hours earlier, at 1:00 PM, Germany's high command had transmitted the password for war, "Dortmund." That afternoon, Hitler had composed letters explaining his decision to attack the Soviet Union to the leaders of Nazi-allied states. Hitler's adjutant Nicolaus von Below noticed that the führer was "increasingly nervous and restless. Hitler talked a lot, walked up and down; he seemed impatient, waiting for something." In his residence in the old Reich Chancellery, Hitler did not sleep for a second straight night. He took a meal in the dining room. He listened to Les Préludes, the symphonic poem by Franz Liszt. He summoned Goebbels, who had just finished watching Gone With the Wind. The two walked up and down Hitler's drawing room for quite a while, finalizing the timing and content of Hitler's war proclamation for the next day, which would focus on "the salvation of Europe" and the intolerable danger of waiting any longer. Goebbels left at 2:30 AM, returning to the Propaganda Ministry, where staff had been told to await him. "Everyone was absolutely astonished," he wrote in his diary, "even though most had guessed half of what was going on, and some all of it." The Germans had given the invasion the code name Operation Barbarossa. Now, it had begun.

Most of the intended recipients in Soviet frontline positions failed to receive Directive Number 1. Wehrmacht advance units, many disguised in Red Army uniforms, had already crossed the border and sabotaged Soviet communications. "The beginning of every war is like opening the door into a dark room," Hitler had told one of his private secretaries. "One never knows what is hidden in the darkness."

A German infantryman walks toward the body of a Soviet soldier and burning Soviet BT-7 tank in the early days of Operation Barbarossa, 1941.

BLINDED BY THE MIGHT

Stalin's regime had reproduced a deep-set pattern in Russian history: Russian rulers launching forced modernizations to overcome or at least manage the asymmetry of a country that considered itself a providential power with a special mission in the world but that substantially lagged behind the other great powers. The urgent quest for a strong state had culminated, once more, in personal rule. Stalin's regime defined the terms of public thought and individual identity, and Stalin himself personified the passions and dreams of a socialist modernity and Soviet might. With single-sentence telegrams or brief phone calls, he could spur the clunky Soviet party-state machinery into action, invoking discipline and intimidation, to be sure, but also galvanizing young functionaries who felt close emotional ties to him and millions more who would never come close to meeting him in person.

Stalin's regime promised not merely statist modernization but also the transcendence of private property and markets, of class antagonisms and existential alienation—a renewal of the social whole rent by the bourgeoisie, a quest for social justice on a global scale. In worldview and practice, it was a conspiracy that perceived conspiracy everywhere and in everything, constantly gaslighting itself. In administration, it constituted a crusade for planning and control that ended up generating a proliferation of improvised illegalities, a perverse drive for order, and a system in which propaganda and myths about "the system" were the most systematized part. Amid the cultivated opacity and patent falsehoods, even most high officials were reduced to Kremlinology. The fanatical hypercentralization was often self-defeating, but the cult of the party's and especially Stalin's infallibility proved to be the most dangerous flaw of Stalin's fallible rule.

By inclination, Stalin was a Russian nationalist in the imperial sense, and anti-Westernism was the core impulse of this longstanding Russian-Eurasian political culture. Initially, the ambitious Soviet quest to match the West had actually increased the country's dependency on Western technology and know-how. But after importing technology from every advanced Western economy, Stalin's regime went on to develop its own sophisticated military and related industries to a degree unprecedented for even a military-first country. Geopolitically, however, whereas tsarist Russia had concluded foreign alliances for its security, the Soviet Union mostly sought, or could manage, only nonaggression pacts. Its sole formal alliance, formed with France, lacked any military dimension. The country's self-isolation became ever more extreme.

Stalin insisted on calling fascism "reactionary," a supposed way for the bourgeoisie to preserve the old world. But Hitler turned out to be someone neither Marx nor Lenin had prepared Stalin for. A lifelong Germanophile, Stalin appears to have been mesmerized by the might and daring of Germany's parallel totalitarian regime. For a time, he recovered his personal and political equilibrium in his miraculous pact with Hitler, which deflected the German war machine, delivered a bounty of German industrial tools, enabled the conquest and Sovietization of tsarist borderlands, and reinserted the Soviet Union into the role of arbitrating world affairs. Hitler had whetted and, reluctantly, abetted Stalin's own appetite. But far earlier than the despot imagined, his ability to extract profit from the immense danger Hitler posed to Europe and the world had run its course. This generated unbearable tension in Stalin's life and rule, yet he stubbornly refused to come to grips with the new realities, and not solely out of greed for German technology. Despite his insight into the human psyche, demonic shrewdness, and sharp mind, Stalin was blinkered by ideology and fixed ideas. British Prime Minister Winston Churchill controlled not a single division on the Soviet frontier, yet Stalin remained absolutely obsessed with British imperialism, railing against the Treaty of Versailles long after Hitler had shredded it and continuing to imagine that Hitler was negotiating with the British behind his back.

HITLER'S CHOICE

For Hitler, the 1939 pact had been a distasteful necessity that, with luck, would not endure very long. His racial, social Darwinist, zero-sum understanding of geopolitics meant that both the Soviet Union and the United Kingdom would have to be annihilated in order for Germany to realize its master-race destiny. To be sure, in the immediate term, he thought in terms of domination of the European continent (Grossmacht), which required Lebensraum—living space—in the east. But in the longer term, he foresaw domination of the world (Weltmacht), which would require a blue-water fleet, bases rimming the Atlantic, and a colonial empire in the tropics for raw materials. That was incompatible with the continued existence of the British Empire, at least in the form it took at that time. Hitler thus put himself in front of a stark choice of either agreeing to deepen the pact with Stalin and taking on the entire British Empire, which would mean conceding at least a partial Soviet sphere in the Balkans and on the Black Sea—on top of the Soviet sphere in the Baltics—or, alternatively, freeing himself from the infuriating dependency on Moscow and taking on the British later. In the end, military circumstances helped determine the sequencing: Hitler did not possess the air or naval capabilities or the depth of resources to prevail militarily over the United Kingdom; he did have the land forces to attempt to smash the Soviet Union.

A commitment to a prolonged contest for supremacy with the British, whom Hitler expected to be aided more and more by the vast resources of the United States, made quick annihilation of the Soviet Union an absolutely necessary prelude. Moreover, even though Hitler and the German high command knew that the Soviet Union was not poised to attack, the invasion amounted to a preventive war all the same in his logic, for the Soviet Union was only getting stronger and might itself attack at a time it deemed more advantageous. And so in 1940, while pushing Japan to attack British positions in East Asia, Hitler had offered the British government a version of the pact he had concluded with Stalin and seemed dumbfounded when the British government did not accept it. The Nazi leader had grasped the British imperial mindset, and he was sincere when promising that, in exchange for a free hand on the continent, he would keep the British Empire intact for now. He continued to hold out hope that the United Kingdom, patently weak militarily on land and therefore unable to defeat him, would come to terms with him. But Hitler had failed to understand the long-standing British preference for a balance of power on the continent (on which the security of the empire, too, partly depended). And he perceived far more common interests between London and Moscow than either of them saw themselves.

Hitler turned out to be someone neither Marx nor Lenin had prepared Stalin for.

During the preparations for the blitzkrieg against the Soviets, Hitler continued to devote resources to preparing for a long naval and air war against the British and the United States. May and June of 1941 was the blackest period yet for the United Kingdom: Germany was sinking its ships and bombing its cities, and it had lost its position in the Balkans. After German paratroopers had captured Crete, in late May 1941, the British position seemed grievously imperiled. Eleven days before the scheduled launch of his Soviet invasion, Hitler had dictated a draft of Directive Number 32, "Preparations for the Time after Barbarossa." It envisioned the subdivision and exploitation of Soviet territories, as well as a pincer movement against the Suez Canal and British positions in the Middle East; the conquest of Gibraltar, northwestern Africa, and the Spanish and Portuguese Atlantic islands, to eliminate the British in the Mediterranean; and the building of coastal bases in West and possibly East Africa. Eventually, there would need to be a German base in Afghanistan for seizing British India.

Had Hitler thrown all his might into this "peripheral strategy" rather than invading the Soviet Union, the United Kingdom might not have survived. The war with the Soviets would have gone ahead at some point, but with the British knocked out of the picture. There would have been no British beachhead to assist an eventual U.S.-led Allied landing in western Europe.

THE WISDOM OF BISMARCK

Hitler cannot be explained in terms of his social origins or his early life and influences, a point that is no less applicable to Stalin. The greatest shaper of Stalin's identity was the building and running of a dictatorship, whereby he assumed responsibility for the Soviet Union's power in the world. In the name of socialism, Stalin, pacing in his Kremlin office, had grown accustomed to moving millions of peasants, workers— whole nations—across a sixth of the earth, on his own initiative, often consulting no one. But his world had become intensely constricted. Hitler had trapped the Soviet despot in his Little Corner.

Stalin's dealings with Hitler differed from British appeasement in that Stalin tried deterrence as well as accommodation. But Stalin's policy resembled British appeasement in that he was driven by a blinding desire to avoid war at all costs. He displayed strength of capabilities but not of will. Neither his fearsome resolve nor his supreme cunning—which had enabled him to vanquish his rivals and spiritually crush his inner circle—was in evidence in 1941. He shrank from trying to preempt Hitler militarily and failed to preempt him diplomatically.

In the end, however, the question of who most miscalculated is not a simple one. "Of all the men who can lay claim to having paved the way" for the Third Reich, Hitler liked to say, "one figure stands in awe-inspiring solitude: Bismarck." But Bismarck had built his chancellorship on avoiding conflict with Russia. When a bust of Bismarck was transferred from the old Reich Chancellery to Hitler's new Reich Chancellery, it had broken off at the neck. A replica was hastily made and artificially aged by soaking it in cold tea. No one shared this omen with Hitler.

STEPHEN KOTKIN is John P. Birkelund '52 Professor in History and International Affairs at Princeton University and a Senior Fellow at the Hoover Institution. This essay is adapted from his most recent book, *Stalin: Waiting for Hitler, 1929–1941* (Penguin Press, 2017), the second in a three-volume biography of the Soviet leader.

How to Counter Fake News

Technology Can Help Distinguish Fact From Fiction

Martin J. O'Malley and Peter L. Levin

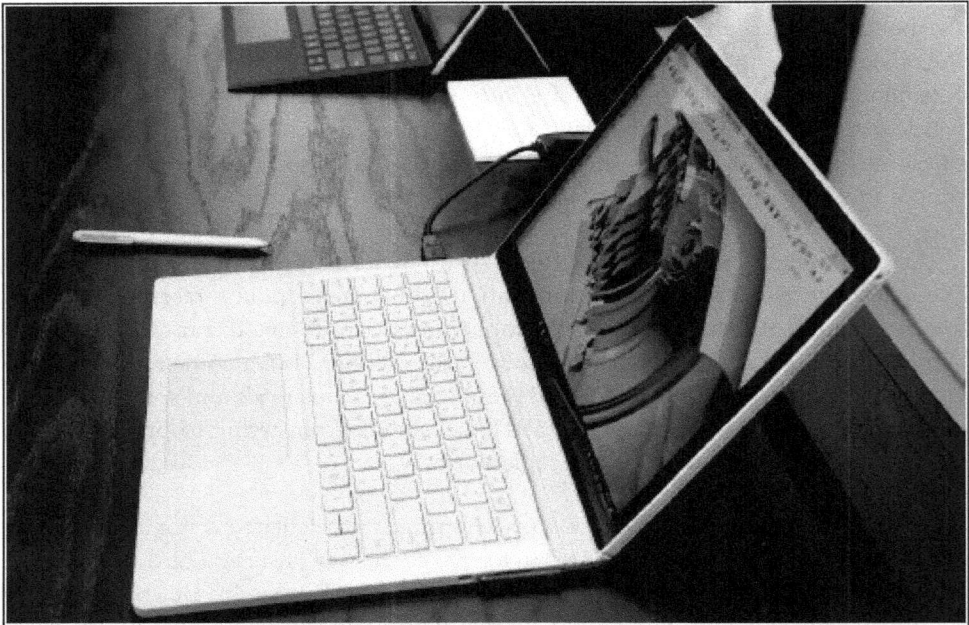

During the 2016 U.S. presidential election, Macedonian teens looking to get paid for ad-clicks, Russian cyber sophisticates apparently looking to tilt the outcome, and some homegrown mood manipulators broadcast outrageous and false stories packaged to look like real news. Their counterfeit posts were nearly indistinguishable from authentic coin and remain so, even in the face of skeptical but impatient fact-checking.

Although much of the establishment has been left wringing its hands about what to do—how to ferret out fake news and those who produce it—there are already tools and systems to help digital investigations and gumshoe reporters connect the dots and discover scams. Metadata—the data about data—can provide a digital signature to identify actors on the Internet. And the Web itself allows us to examine timelines, serialize events, and identify primary sources. Some signatures are harder to find than others, but they are all there; you just need to know where to look and what to analyze.

Indeed, the intelligence community already thwarts terrorist attacks through methods like these, known in the vernacular as "tools, processes, and procedures," and the Department of Homeland Security maintains a knowledge center of vulnerabilities. Such work will be aided by the newly created Global Engagement Center, (section 1287 of the National Defense Authorization Act signed by U.S. President Barack Obama just before Christmas), which expands the government's repertoire and mandate to "identify current and emerging trends in foreign propaganda and disinformation in order to coordinate and shape the development of tactics, techniques, and procedures to expose and refute foreign misinformation and disinformation and proactively promote fact-based narratives and policies to audiences outside the United States."

The language comes from a cybersecurity bill that U.S. Senator Rob Portman (R-Ohio) introduced last spring. According to co-sponsor Chris Murphy (D-Conn.), the United States now has dedicated "resources to confront our adversaries' widespread efforts to spread false narratives that undermine democratic institutions and compromise America's foreign policy goals" in the digital age. With modest funding and proper oversight, the Global Engagement Center will help the government reach back in time and across virtual space to ensure that streams of data are not contaminated by state-sponsored misinformation or falsehoods.

The center's special envoy and coordinator, Michael Lumpkin, told us that it

---

is an agile, innovative, data-driven organization, and this is precisely the approach needed to take on the emerging threats in the information space. Unfortunately, the State Department is not known for agility or innovation. Too often we are using nineteenth century bureaucracy, with twentieth century technology to fight twenty first century adversaries. We simply have to get better in the information battlespace. We've made progress since ISIS first came onto the world stage, but as the challenges and adversaries morph, agility will continue to be key.

There are other steps Washington and the media can take now, born of Portman's legislation, network architecture, and operational practices, which would protect the public.

In November, Merrimack College media professor Melissa Zimdars posted some tips for analyzing news sources. Her report was followed last month by Silicon Valley publisher Tim O'Reilly's outline of a basic verification framework that chronicles the steps he took to fact-check an Internet "meme" that claimed to correlate crime rates to voting trends. The story was easily proved false, but doing so required personal persistence and the ability to make creative connections between authentic root sources. Few people could, or would, invest the amount of time that Zimdars or O'Reilly recommend, but computers are not intimidated by a mountain of pattern-matching tasks. Indeed, O'Reilly's framework is ripe for automation. From a technological perspective, these are surprisingly easy problems to address, and we can do so safely, securely, and reliably.

Today almost 40 percent of Americans get their news online. A "we report, you decide" approach to truth undermines a critical feedback loop that makes democratic governance possible. If the most reputable news organizations do not invest time and treasure in confirming sources and facts, then representative democracy becomes a mayhem of funhouse mirrors.

But the Internet is constructed to resist obstructions. Picture water flowing around rocks in a river. Place a big boulder in the middle, and the current will divert around it, although the water level may rise in the vicinity of the blockage. In this analogy, the drops of water are data packets, and Internet packets are designed to remember the precise path they take to keep the aggregate flow manageable and predictable.

Consequently, network gateways—the tributaries to and channels from the aggregate flow—can always determine where a message originates. Although it is impossible to predict what will happen downstream, it is easy to know how many and which nodes a packet passed through on its way from its source to a waypoint. Indeed, in much the same way that we "authenticate" people we can hear but not see—by their phone number, by the sound of their voice, by their vocabulary, by their interests—so too can we authenticate real news. We can do this by generating (through machine learning or by brute-force pattern-matching) a signature that reconstructs the flow of a packet. We can examine the waypoints of the packets between source and destination to determine its origin (a proxy for authenticity), and we can patiently maintain a record of trustworthy signatures over time. In that way technology can quickly distinguish between uncontaminated springs of news and manufactured springs that have been poisoned with misinformation or disinformation.

Of course, attribution and anonymity are zero-sum. And not even an intelligent machine will sort perfectly. But for now, the problem is that identifying fake news is a manual process prone to human error and the duress of news-cycle urgency. As long as media and readers are unable to quickly and reliably expose fake news, it will undermine the public's ability to govern itself. And the inability to unmask state-sponsored Internet propaganda could well pose a very real threat to national security. That is why even an imperfect automated sorting process is better than nothing.

The inability to unmask state-sponsored Internet propaganda could well pose a very real threat to national security.

The scourge of misinformation is as old as language itself, but Internet-fast global manipulation is relatively new. The good news is that there are methods and systems that can help ordinary users discern what's reliable from what's invented. Major distribution platforms—from network and cable news to web-based platforms that service billions of users—should move quickly toward sensible solutions that do not censor, but that do provide citizen consumers with a qualitative indication of reliability. Software applications will learn how to do this, much like they already, if imperfectly, catch spam in email.

"Trust but verify" is a serviceable policy framework when there's plausible reason to trust, and ready means to verify. The erosion of these traditional norms on the Internet scuttles authentic debate on the rocks of superstition, impulse, emotion, and bias. With new public-sector investment and private-sector innovation, we are optimistic that the United States can fight back against fake news and foreign influence in U.S. elections.

MARTIN J. O'MALLEY is a former two-term Governor of Maryland and two-term Mayor of Baltimore. He was a Democratic candidate for president in 2016. PETER L. LEVIN is Adjunct Senior Fellow in the Technology and National Security program at the Center for a New American Security, and CEO of Amida Technology Solutions, Inc.

Trump Takes Aim at the European Union

Why the EU Won't Unify In Response

Kathleen R. McNamara

U.S. President Donald Trump in the White House, January 2017.

A few days before his inauguration as U.S. president, Donald J. Trump took aim at the United States' most important allies. In an interview co-published by Germany's Bild and The Times of London on January 15, Trump disparaged NATO as "obsolete," chastised German Chancellor Angela Merkel for her government's openness to asylum seekers, and seemed to advocate the breakup of the European Union, calling it a "vehicle for Germany." Those comments came two days after a different bombshell: on January 13, Anthony Gardner, the outgoing U.S. ambassador to the EU, said that officials from Trump's transition team had called EU leaders and asked which EU country would be "leaving next."

Trump's words marked an extraordinary departure from the norms of the postwar transatlantic relationship. For decades, the United States and the EU have been each other's most important foreign policy partners, tightly bound by a thicket of alliances and institutions, joined at the hip in promoting liberal democratic values, and trading and investing with each other at unprecedented levels. Particularly in light of the uncertainties surrounding the United Kingdom's exit from the EU, Trump's comments shocked many observers who support the transatlantic relationship and the broader liberal order it guarantees.

Might Trump's attacks backfire by encouraging EU countries to unify against him? A number of European leaders have suggested as much. "We Europeans have our fate in our own hands," Merkel said on January 16, in a forceful response to Trump's comments. Others have echoed French Finance Minister Michel Sapin, who said on January 17 that "the more [Trump] makes this sort of statement, the more Europeans close ranks."

Unfortunately for supporters of the European project, Sapin's prediction is unlikely to hold. Instead of unifying the EU, Trump's apparent Euroskepticism may undermine it by stirring up popular anger against internal enemies: the faceless EU technocrats and disdained national elites who seem disconnected from the day-to-day problems of most European people.

Peter Macdiarmid / REUTERS

At a demonstration against the Iraq war in London, February 2003.

LIKE NO OTHER

What are the reasons to believe that Trump's presidency might prompt the EU's revival? The first is that people tend to define their identities not only in reference to those with whom they share values and cultures but also in opposition to those with whom they do not. Social psychologists have long argued that the construction of a sharply drawn other encourages group solidarity. At first glance, it appears that Trump could play precisely that role.

The West has certainly seen that kind of dynamic before. Consider the Europe-wide antiwar demonstrations that took place on February 15, 2003, in Athens, Helsinki, London, Madrid, Paris, and Rome, when millions marched against then President George W. Bush and the imminent U.S. invasion of Iraq. Citizens across the EU reviled Bush for what they viewed as his illiberal warmongering and rejection of international treaties on climate change and human rights. European intellectuals such as Jacques Derrida and Jürgen Habermas heralded the protests as evidence of a newly united continent.

Much has happened since then to weaken European solidarity. A global financial crisis and soaring income inequality have brought economic stagnation to millions on both sides of the Atlantic. Many Europeans now view the EU as either the source of the problem (especially in the countries most hurt by the eurozone crisis) or as an accessory to it, and they blame EU policies supporting open borders and the free movement of people for much of Europe's malaise. The increasingly popular argument that the EU is governed by technocratic experts and establishment party elites who are out of touch with the people is giving populists all the material they need to win at the ballot box, as was the case with the Brexit vote.

Trump may seem more like an ally than like an other.

In this context, Trump may seem more like an ally than like an other. That is why many of Europe's populist leaders, including the heads of France's National Front and Italy's Five Star Movement and Northern League, have embraced the new U.S. president. (So has the British Conservative Party, the only centrist party in the EU to have done so.)

But if the United States cannot play the role of a unifying other for the EU, perhaps there is another way that Trump's jabs could solidify the bloc. Political unification feeds on threats: most of today's nation-states were formed when governments centralized political and administrative power in order to survive serious dangers, such as wars. What is more, political communities often rally around the flag and solidify their national identities during apparent crises.

Here again, the answer to whether Trump could unify the EU should offer only lukewarm comfort to the union's supporters. Trump's inflammatory comments do not pose an immediate existential threat to the bloc. If the entente between Trump and Russian President Vladimir Putin proves enduring and inflicts direct harm on Europe's interests, that may change, and Europeans may find themselves forced to unify in response. But even if that dynamic materializes, its effects might be drowned out by popular demands for political change after years of economic austerity and technocratic leadership.

Michaela Rehle / REUTERS

German Chancellor Angela Merkel and French President Francois Hollande in Ludwigsburg, Germany, September 2012.

FEW SILVER LININGS

The imagined community of Europeans that the EU has constructed offers only watered-down versions of the cultural and emotional attachments of traditional nationalism. The threats that Trump may present to the EU are therefore unlikely to bring about an immediate or heartfelt embrace of the European project. Instead, his stance may encourage the kind of authoritarian populism that has already taken hold in Hungary and Poland.

The EU and the transatlantic liberal order that Trump recently attacked were created to advance American interests at a time when the United States had unsurpassed power. Out of the ashes of World War II, the United States approved the constitution for postwar West Germany, helped bring about the birth of the EU, constructed the foundations of what would eventually become the World Trade Organization, and drew up the blueprint for NATO. These liberal institutions, created in the United States' image, acted as a bulwark against the Soviet Union and underwrote prosperity and stability, guaranteeing the same kinds of American wealth and power that Trump has promised to restore.

The EU's road ahead is steep. As it manages the consequences of Trump's election, it must also face its own shortcomings. EU leaders and citizens must confront the passions of populism head on, responding with a full-throated defense of the EU's achievements while building the capacity at both the national and European levels to deal with the union's challenges. As for the United States, it may be in a deeper hole, since it must confront the possibility that many of the institutions that have historically underpinned its supremacy may be dismantled. For the EU, that prospect offers few silver linings.

KATHLEEN R. MCNAMARA is Professor of Government and Foreign Service at Georgetown University and the author of *The Politics of Everyday Europe: Constructing Authority in the European Union*. Follow her on Twitter @ProfKMcNamara.

© Foreign Affairs

Good Foreign Policy Is Invisible

Why Boring Is Better

James Goldgeier and Elizabeth N. Saunders

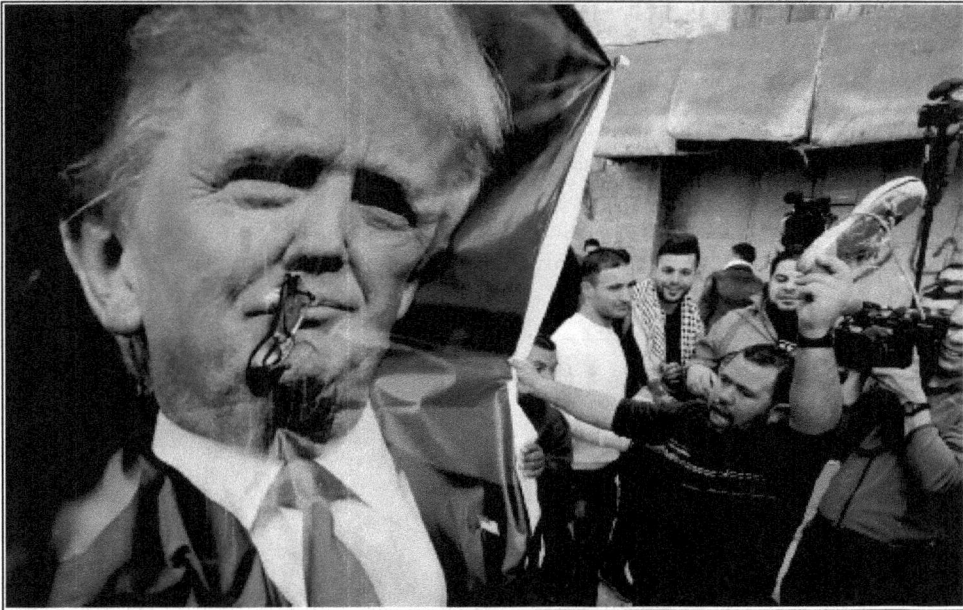

A Palestinian demonstrator throws a shoe on a poster depicting U.S. President Donald Trump during a protest in the West Bank city of Hebron February 24, 2017.

In his quest to Make America Great Again by putting America First, U.S. President Donald Trump spent his first weeks in office disrupting relations with allies and adversaries alike. He complained to the Australian prime minister about what he called the "dumb deal" the United States made in agreeing to relocate approximately 1,250 refugees from Australia to the United States; he suggested to the Mexican president that the United States might help take care of some "tough hombres" there; and he declared to French President François Hollande that the United States should get its "money back" for its years as NATO's leader. He apparently also remains determined to enact an executive order temporarily banning immigration from seven Muslim-majority countries despite the early judicial rulings against his efforts.

Micah Zenko and Rebecca Lissner, from the Council on Foreign Relations, have described Trump's approach to foreign policy as "tactical transactionalism," that is "a foreign-policy framework that seeks discrete wins (or the initial tweet-able impression of them), treats foreign relations bilaterally rather than multidimensionally, and resists the alignment of means and ends that is necessary for effective grand strategy."

But the problem isn't just about any one deal. It isn't even Trump's lack of an overall grand strategy. The problem is that successful foreign policy is largely invisible. It often means paying up front for benefits that are hard to see until you lose them, or that will only be obvious when you really need them. Sometimes, successful foreign policy even means keeping real victories quiet.

Invisible foreign policy doesn't appeal to a president who cares about showmanship and flashy successes. Although Trump's initial storm of activity seems to have calmed in recent days, there is no evidence that he has turned to the kind of quiet, routine actions that make U.S. foreign policy run smoothly. Such efforts are not dramatic, but they are essential, and their absence could severely undermine U.S. interests.

KEVIN LAMARQUE / REUTERS

U.S. President Donald Trump speaks during his meeting with health insurance company CEOs at the White House in Washington, February 27, 2017.

INVISIBLE BENEFITS ARE BORING

The policies that Trump decries have something in common. Free trade, alliances, and non-splashy diplomacy all come with public costs and less visible benefits. For example, free-trade agreements make it cheaper for everyone to buy consumer goods like televisions; but because such a benefit is spread out among all Americans, any given shopper at Best Buy is not likely to give the free-trade agreements themselves much thought. They certainly notice, however, the costs when a factory closes down in their town.

Trade restrictions have the opposite effect: the "Buy America" policies Trump advocates could increase costs for a broad swath of the American public. As has been widely reported, a survey of the ingredients of Trump-branded goods reveals that even Trump himself doesn't think that buying American is always the best deal for American entrepreneurs.

Economists have long understood the concentrated costs and diffuse benefits of trade, which make costs politically salient and benefits harder to sell. Less obvious is that the benefits of alliances and diplomacy are also largely invisible. The only kind of diplomacy Trump ever talks about is deal making, but a better analogy for most diplomacy is preventive care: it's incremental and it involves tending to allies, trading partners, and other strategically important countries. Alliances and diplomatic relationships are like insurance: however badly you need them in a crisis, you can only access them if you've been paying your premiums all along.

Preventive alliance care is boring but essential. The benefits are hard to measure (although the New York Times recently made a valiant attempt to quantify what the United States gets out of its alliances: we do $699 billion in trade with our European Union partners alone), but if the alliances disappear, there will be big and obvious costs.

Regular diplomacy also functions this way: most diplomatic visits abroad by the president and secretary of state are not to secure major deals, but rather to reinforce or maintain existing diplomatic partnerships. The apparent marginalization of Secretary of State Rex Tillerson from Trump's decision-making and public diplomacy would make sense only to a president who views diplomacy as marginal.

THIS ONE WEIRD TRICK HAS GIVEN AMERICA PEACE AND PROSPERITY

Thomas Schelling, the Nobel Prize–winning scholar who passed away late last year, noted that all of us tend to prioritize short-term gratification over long-term benefits. This means, as Schelling described, that "many of us have little tricks we play on ourselves to make us do the things we ought to do or to keep us from the things we have foresworn."

The liberal international order has been American foreign policy's most important trick for paying attention to the long term (at least since the end of World War II). Elites have agreed that a liberalizing trade environment, a robust network of alliances, and regularized diplomacy provide worthwhile benefits.

In addition to providing benefits that are hard to see, such as the lower costs of goods thanks to trade, this trick also stops policymakers engaging in policies like protectionism that seem like a quick win but can be seriously damaging. The Smoot-Hawley tariff was introduced in 1930 to protect the U.S. economy from foreign competition, but it ended up prolonging the Great Depression. After this dismal experience, the Reciprocal Trade Agreements Act (RTAA) changed the institutional blueprint according to which American trade policy was set. The new format helped make protectionism easier to resist by giving the president advance authority from Congress to negotiate trade agreements, lowering the requirement for congressional approval to a simple majority rather than a majority of two-thirds, and tying U.S. tariff reductions to reciprocal foreign tariff cuts, all of which generated increasingly durable political support for free trade.

Alliances and day-to-day diplomacy force policymakers and the public to pay the premiums on insurance policies that they may need when things get tough. They have also helped keep major wars at bay for 70 years, both directly, through good relationships with allies and partners, and indirectly, through the balance of power that strong alliances help reinforce.

This is one reason why Trump's berating of Australian Prime Minister Malcolm Turnbull was so shocking. Critics—including many former GOP foreign policy officials—pointed out that Australia has been a staunch U.S. ally, contributing troops to nearly all the conflicts in which the United States has been involved since World War I, including the 2003 Iraq War. Australia's contributions to conflicts in Asia—over 17,000 Australians served in the Korean War and over 60,000 in the Vietnam War—are an important reminder of Australia's importance to the United States' future position in Asia in the face of a rising China.

An activist paints the U.S.-Mexico border wall between Ciudad Juarez and New Mexico as a symbol of protest against U.S. President Donald Trump's new immigration reform in Ciudad Juarez, Mexico February 26, 2017.

To be sure, most Democratic and Republican foreign policy elites still back a version of the liberal international order, but they need to step up as Trump challenges it. Indeed, there are important pockets of support even within Trump's administration. Both Tillerson and James Mattis, Trump's new secretaries of state and defense, respectively, voiced strong support for NATO during their confirmation hearings, despite the president's assertion that the alliance is "obsolete"; and Vice President Mike Pence voiced strong support for NATO at this year's Munich Security Conference.

DON'T BLAME THE PUBLIC

Usually, when we worry about domestic support for the international order, we're worried about public opinion (for example, scholars have debated whether public support for the international order has eroded, particularly in an era of partisan polarization). However, Trump's rise is not simply a story of popular revolt against the liberal order. Even people's views about trade, which can affect jobs and wages, do not necessarily track cleanly with their economic self-interest. Rather, trade preferences often reflect economic or social anxieties—in other words, they are shaped by many of the same forces that drove the presidential vote, rather than by the specifics of trade policy.

Most voters probably weren't thinking much about alliances and diplomacy when they cast their ballots, but even if they had, it's doubtful they would train their fire on longtime U.S. partners, as Trump has done in his first few weeks. Indeed, as the Times reported, in a survey conducted just before the revelation of the troublesome Australia call, respondents were asked to rate whether countries were allies or enemies of the United States. Among Republicans, the country that came out top on the list of allies? Australia.

Trump made these issues salient by weaving a campaign narrative around concerns about Americans losing jobs due to free-trade deals and paying too much to support rich allies. He then wrapped these issues up in rhetoric about the most egregious mistakes elites have made in recent years, most notably the Iraq war debacle and the 2008 financial crisis, to seek to convince the public that a new approach was necessary seven decades after the end of World War II.

In short, the source of today's attack on international order is not the public, nor is it partisan elites, but rather it is the president himself, with White House adviser Steve Bannon by his side. All this will severely complicate any efforts to restore faith in the order. It is not merely a problem of better messaging—it will always be difficult to get voters roused about something as abstract as the liberal international order.

Instead, it's up to those elites who still recognize and prioritize the invisible benefits that the system has provided to protect or promote it. Those inside Trump's administration, such as Tillerson, Mattis, and recently appointed National Security Advisor H.R. McMaster, as well as their few allies in Congress—particularly in the Republican Party—can play a key part if they are willing to take the risk, and if Trump gives them a hearing.

Someone will have to tell Trump to take a trip to Germany without the expectation of bringing home a deal. Someone will have to remind him that strong alliances with Australia, Japan, and South Korea will be useful if there is a confrontation with China, especially since China itself lacks allies. Someone will have to point out to Trump that trade protection leads to price hikes at Walmart.

These same elites may also have to remind Trump that some foreign policy victories need to stay invisible—that he won't be able take public credit for some of them. Crisis stability, terrorism prevention, intelligence gathering, and many other aspects of foreign policy are largely about the dogs that didn't bark, the project that takes time to bear fruit, or the story that must stay secret until some day far in the future.

Elites still need to confront the criticisms of the existing order that Trump has exploited. The costs of free trade do fall disproportionately on some Americans; Council on Foreign Relations trade expert Edward Alden has detailed the failure of every administration since John F. Kennedy's to deliver on promised trade adjustment assistance to workers left behind by increasing globalization. NATO allies do need to get serious about spending a minimum of 2 percent of their GDP on defense, as they have pledged to do (only Estonia, Greece, Poland, the United Kingdom and the United States manage)—not because meeting the target would have major defense implications, but rather to maintain political support from NATO's chief benefactor.

The track record of the postwar international order has been written in invisible ink. But it is remarkably strong. If we are not successful in defending it, its benefits may finally become plain to see—precisely because they are gone.

JAMES GOLDGEIER is Dean of the School of International Service at American University.

ELIZABETH N. SAUNDERS is Associate Professor of Political Science and International Affairs at George Washington University.

© Foreign Affairs

The Coming Islamic Culture War

What the Middle East's Internet Boom Means for Gay Rights, and More

Daveed Gartenstein-Ross and Nathaniel Barr

Filipino Muslim children pray before a lesson at a Manila mosque, June 2014.

Western observers are often blind to social currents within the Muslim world. During the Arab Spring revolutions of 2011, outside analysts confidently predicted that the uprisings would marginalize the jihadist movement in favor of more moderate and democratic reformers. In fact, the opposite happened—an unprecedented jihadist mobilization that has inspired legions of fighters from around the world and fragmented or threatened more than half a dozen countries. In large part, this was because the collapse of the old regimes, which had suppressed Islamism domestically, created new spaces for jihadists. These spaces included both literal ungoverned territory and discursive spaces, where radicals were newly able to engage in dawa, or proselytism.

Today, a new type of discursive space—one that will foster a very different set of ideas—is opening up in the Muslim world. In April 2011, Bahraini human rights activists created one such space when they launched the website Ahwaa, the first online forum for the LGBT community in the Middle East and North Africa (MENA) region. Esra'a al-Shafei, one of the website's founders, was modest about the site's ambitions, explaining that Ahwaa was intended "as a support network" for the "LGBTQ community" as well as a resource for those "who want to learn more by interacting with [LGBT] people."

Although little-noticed at the time, Ahwaa's seemingly innocuous project was in fact revolutionary. Homosexuality in the MENA region is not only stigmatized but generally criminalized and banished from the public sphere. The creation of an online platform where LGBT people could candidly discuss the issues affecting their lives, such as romantic relationships or the tensions between Islam and gay rights, was thus a direct challenge to deeply inscribed cultural and religious norms. Indeed, Ahwaa heralds a wave of challenging ideas that, fueled by rapidly rising Internet penetration, will soon inundate Muslim-majority countries.

Online communications, by their nature, give marginalized social and political groups a space to organize, mobilize, and ultimately challenge the status quo. In the MENA region, online spaces like Awhaa will give sexual minorities the ability to assert their identity, rights, and place in society. So too will the Internet amplify discourses critical of the Islamic faith, or of religion in general, and solidify the identities of secularists, atheists, and even apostates. The rise of these religion-critical discourses will in turn trigger a backlash from conservative forces who fear an uprooting of traditional beliefs and identities. The coming social tsunami should be visible to anyone who knows what signs to look for.

THE INTERNET BOOM

The past two decades in the West have seen an extraordinarily rapid revolution in LGBT rights. In 1996, Democratic President Bill Clinton signed into law the Defense of Marriage Act, which defined marriage as the union between one man and one woman. While running for president twelve years later, in 2008, Democratic nominee Barack Obama was still defending this definition, adding, "I'm not somebody who promotes same-sex marriage." But public opinion on the issue shifted rapidly. By 2011, more people supported gay marriage than opposed it. And by the time Obama left office, not only was same-sex marriage a constitutionally protected right, but it was inconceivable that a viable Democratic candidate would oppose it. Indeed, the transformation has affected both sides of the aisle—current President Donald Trump is doubtless the most pro-LGBT Republican nominee of all time.

The rise in Internet access was central to this revolution. Joe Kapp, an LGBT-identifying entrepreneur, has written about how the revolution in online communications "allowed LGBT people to bridge disparate geographies," to "safely and discreetly find partners," and to "learn that they are not alone, regardless of where they live." The increasing confidence and visibility of LGBT people allowed them to move the needle on gay marriage, first incrementally and then more assertively as public opinion began to shift. As Kapp writes, "One need only look at the sea of red equal signs that appeared on Facebook in support of marriage equality to see the potential impact of sharing ideas across new social media."

Access to the Internet is now growing rapidly outside the West. In Muslim-majority countries Internet penetration rates, which measure the percentage of a country's population with Internet access, have long lagged behind those of the developed world—but this state of affairs is changing. In 2010, according to Internet World Stats, Internet penetration rates in sub-Saharan Africa and the Middle East were just 10.9 percent and 29.8 percent, respectively. In North America, by contrast, the rate stood at 77.4 percent. But by 2016 Internet penetration had risen to 28 percent in sub-Saharan Africa and 57 percent in the Middle East. Indeed, some Muslim countries have been at the forefront of the global boom in Internet access—Saudi Arabia's rate more than doubled from 2007 to 2016, and Tunisia's rate over the same period went from 13 percent to just under 50 percent.

Amr Dalsh / Reuters

A mosque at sunset in Cairo, October 2016.

This boom is occurring in some of the most conservative societies on Earth, where ideas contrary to or critical of a strict interpretation of Islam are often stigmatized or even punished. With regard to sexuality, for instance, most Muslim societies consider discussions of homosexuality and LGBT rights to be off-limits. Indeed, most institutionalize anti-LGBT discrimination through their legal systems. Homosexual acts are illegal in all Muslim-majority MENA countries, with the exception of Jordan and Bahrain. Several states deem homosexuality an offense punishable by death. In addition to state violence, LGBT-identifying individuals can also be threatened by vigilantes. In 2014, for example, a Pakistani man killed three gay men he had met online, explaining that he had done so to send a message about the "evils" of homosexuality.

Throughout the region, conservative religious authorities have played a critical role in shaping public attitudes and establishing social norms around homosexuality. In 2007, a member of the Algerian Ministry of Religious Affairs described homosexuality as an "inversion against nature that has to be cured." Prominent Qatar-based preacher Yusuf Qaradawi has described homosexuality as a "perverted act," and endorsed the killing of homosexuals. This is the same Qaradawi that Georgetown University scholar John Esposito has praised for his "reformist interpretation of Islam"—a testament to the extent to which anti-gay clerical discourses have been normalized in Muslim-majority countries.

It is thus little wonder that people critical of religion, such as apostates, atheists, and blasphemers, are similarly stigmatized. A 2016 Pew Research Center report found that 18 of the 20 countries in the MENA region have criminalized blasphemy, while 14 have banned apostasy. So powerful is the stigma against apostasy that when Egypt's Dar al-Ifta, an official religious institution, announced that there were 866 atheists in the country—a remarkably precise and also laughably low figure—the institution's clerics warned that the figure should "set alarm bells ringing."

Even in countries with relatively lenient legal regimes, such as Lebanon, discourse critical of religion is limited. Vigilante violence can imperil atheists, and sometimes even those who defend religious freedom. Salman Taseer, the former governor of Pakistan's Punjab province, was a courageous and vociferous critic of his country's blasphemy law, describing it at one point as "a law which gives an excuse to extremists and reactionaries to target weak people and minorities." For his stance on the issue, Taseer was gunned down in January 2011 by his own bodyguard, Mumtaz Qadri, a committed Islamist.

Public rage followed Taseer's assassination, but a significant portion of it was directed at the murdered governor rather than his killer. The Pakistani religious organization Jamaat Ahle Sunnat—which is regarded as mainstream and non-extremist—issued a statement warning that "there should be no expression of grief or sympathy on the death of the governor, as those who support blasphemy of the prophet are themselves indulging in blasphemy." When Qadri went to trial, lawyers showered him with rose petalsas he walked into the courthouse. Qadri was hailed as a hero by tens of thousands of demonstrators after the state executed him, and today a shrine has been erected at his gravesite in Islamabad.

In such a hostile environment, both critics of religion and members of the LGBT community are often forced to remain in the shadows. For reasons of legality and personal safety, being too loud can be a bad idea. The growth in Internet penetration will change this dynamic.

For reasons of legality and personal safety, being too loud can be a bad idea. The growth in Internet penetration will change this dynamic.

COMING OUT

Publicly disclosing one's LGBT has long been known as "coming out," a phrase that deliberately invokes a debutante's coming-out party, in which an upper-class young woman is formally introduced into adult society. Reviewing the relevant social-science literature, a recent article in the Journal of Child and Family Studies noted that coming out "has been described as an essential component in [LGBT] identity formation and integration," and carries a variety of mental health benefits related to improved self-esteem and reduced anxiety. Conversely, coming out can result in exposure to discrimination and rejection by friends and family.

In terms of the social stigma it invites, leaving the Islamic faith can also be seen as a kind of coming out, albeit one generally devoid of the celebration that often accompanies outwardly accepting one's LGBT identity. In his book The Apostates, a study of Muslims who leave their religion, British criminologist Simon Cottee recounts the story of a young Sudanese woman who explained that for the individual apostate, leaving Islam is "such an intense journey." To "everyone else," however, "it's just another story, people don't really care." (Cottee noted that by "everyone else," she was referring to non-religious friends of hers; to her family, "it isn't just another story. It is a calamity.")

A Muslim student protests a concert by the gay singer Adam Lambert in Malaysia, October 2010.

Yet for both marginalized groups, the Internet boom will accelerate the process of coming out. Whereas offline space is hostile, online space offers a relatively safe environment where people can assemble, interact, and build relationships. Shielded by the relative anonymity of online communications, marginalized individuals of all stripes can discuss intimate and controversial issues. The Internet, furthermore, allows like-minded people from disparate corners of the world to find one another and create virtual communities. An atheist living in rural Egypt, for example, may not know anyone else who shares his views. But when he goes online, he will find millions of people who do.

To appreciate the impact that increased Internet penetration will have on religiously conservative societies, it is crucial to understand how online interaction changes the behavior of members of marginalized communities. One important theory, that of "identity demarginalization," is particularly instructive. The psychologists Katelyn McKenna and John Bargh, in their 1998 study "Coming Out in the Age of the Internet," coined the term identity demarginalization to explain how people with marginalized and concealable identities (in other words, stigmatized identities that cannot be discerned just by looking at someone) interact with one another online. They found that people with marginalized sexual and political views highly valued the opinions of peers in their online social networks. The online community, for them, became a critical source of emotional support, where people could "for the first time… reap the benefits of joining a group of similar others."

Members of marginalized groups come to more fully embrace their marginalized identities as they engage online with other like-minded people. As one 2008 study on online pro-anorexic groups noted, online forums are "an ideal space for maintaining and validating" a marginalized identity. Perhaps most importantly, McKenna and Bargh concluded that once their identities were demarginalized, people began to consider revealing their identity publicly.

Members of marginalized groups come to more fully embrace their marginalized identities as they engage online with other like-minded people.

MOVING OFFLINE

Marginalized communities in the MENA region have not yet mastered the online environment, but they recognize the promise of digital engagement. As Ahwaa's founder explained, the Internet has functioned as a "gateway to freedom of speech, particularly around taboo topics that face widespread censorship." LGBT activists in North Africa, for instance, have established niche online magazines. Online dating in particular has flourished. Amir Ashour, an Iraqi activist, recalled that when he set out to establish Iraq's first LGBT organization, he gauged interest by using social media, reaching out to personal contacts, and contacting people through Grindr and Tinder, two dating apps.

MENA-based atheists have similarly begun carving out a foothold on social media. Several atheist groups on Facebook have amassed over 20,000 members. These groups have been targeted by conservatives, who have launched coordinated online harassment campaigns designed to get Facebook to suspend atheist accounts. One tactic has involved posting pornographic images to atheist pages, then immediately reporting the images to Facebook. Some Islamists have also reported atheists for allegedly Islamophobic hate speech. These tactics have yielded temporary results: In February 2016, Facebook suspended at least nine atheist groups with a combined following of over 128,000 members, although the social media company quickly restored the pages.

Despite these efforts to silence the online atheist community, the Internet remains a refuge. An atheist from Saudi Arabia, which has criminalized "calling for atheist thought in any form," explained in an interview that Saudi atheists use Facebook and Twitter both to engage in discussions about secularism and religion and to set up in-person underground meetings. The man, who went by a pseudonym, noted that he had met atheists in their forties and fifties, who had only recently revealed their views after interacting with younger atheists online.

Some atheist activists have even begun to operate online under their real names, eschewing the pseudonyms that many still use for protection. In 2013, Egyptian atheists created the Black Ducks YouTube channel, which profiles atheists and other non-religious people from the Arab world. Individuals involved with the channel have made a conscious decision not to mask their identities. As one activist explained, "If we atheists stop being ghosts and materialize, we will be taken more seriously… We'll never get what we want if we don't have the courage to claim it with our real names and faces."

A woman records with her iPad during an anti-government protest in Bahrain, January 2012.

Online discourse within the LGBT community has also evolved and grown bolder, as can be seen in the case of the Ahwaa forum. Members use Ahwaa as a sounding board to discuss a range of sensitive subjects that are rarely broached in public. One individual who self-identified as a lesbian, for example, asked forum members whether homosexuality was forbidden (haram) in Islam, and explained that she felt "so bad just thinking that God didn't even talk about who we are in the Quran." In another thread, a poster explained that he had lost all his friends when he came out to them. The post prompted a wave of sympathetic responses, as forum members comforted the man and offered to befriend him online. Such interactions build social cohesion within the LGBT community and help to strip away stigmas.

But perhaps the most telling thread on Ahwaa relates to a more visible type of identity demarginalization: coming out. In a long discussion ranging over dozens of posts, forum members debated the merits of revealing their sexual orientation to coworkers, friends, and family. Several posters shared their divergent experiences of coming out. One woman warned that she had experienced hardship when she came out to her religiously conservative family, while another woman explained that when she told her mother she was pansexual, her mother initially expressed doubts but ultimately said, "I just want you to be happy." In a separate thread, a girl explained that she lived with "constant fear and guilt" because she kept her sexual identity hidden from her family. Several forum members addressed her concerns. One told her, "do not feel guilty at all. This is who you are, and if you[r] parents cannot understand and would not understand, then you will just have to keep it to yourself. There's no shame in being different." Few comments better exemplify the role that online communities can play in destigmatizing marginalized identities.

CLASHING IDENTITIES

As LGBT and religion-critical communities in Muslim countries become increasingly assertive, they are likely to trigger a backlash from conservative religious forces. Indeed, the backlash has already begun, sometimes violently, at both the state and the sub-state level.

Even as Islamist groups have launched reporting campaigns to shut down atheist Facebook accounts, governments have arrested atheists who are vocal online. In 2015, Egyptian courts sentenced a 21-year-old student to three years in prison after he declared on Facebook that he was an atheist. Saudi Arabia has imprisoned blogger Raif Badawi since 2012 on charges of insulting Islam online, occasionally dragging him out of jail for a public lashing. And across the MENA region, governments have similarly targeted members of the LGBT community who are active online. On dating apps, Egyptian police have used catfishing—a tactic in which individuals use false personas to establish online relationships—to identify and arrest gay men.

In the most extreme cases, members of these marginalized groups have been the victims of targeted sub-state violence. Since 2013, Islamist militants in Bangladesh, some of whom are linked to al-Qaeda in the Indian Subcontinent, have carried out a series of assassinations targeting atheist bloggers. And in April 2016, a jihadist faction pledging allegiance to the Islamic State claimed responsibility for killing the editor of Bangladesh's only LGBT magazine.

WHAT'S NEXT

It is not entirely clear how the Internet-enabled rise of marginalized communities—such as the LGBT or religion-critical ones—will reshape Muslim-majority societies. In the short term, the rise of these social movements may provide a boon to jihadist groups, who often cast themselves as the only force capable of protecting the faith against Western and secular values. But over the long term, these marginalized groups may fundamentally challenge religious conservatives' grip on power.

This could produce sweeping social and policy changes—similar, perhaps, to what we have witnessed with respect to the issue of gay marriage in the United States. But it could also generate massive social instability, akin to the tumult of the Arab Uprisings, and the attendant failure to put countries like Libya back together.

Regardless of their ultimate outcome, however, signs of the coming Islamic culture wars can already be discerned. Western observers have long overlooked or misinterpreted social trends that have swept through Muslim-majority countries. This is one trend that they cannot afford to miss.

DAVEED GARTENSTEIN-ROSS is Senior Fellow at the Foundation for Defense of Democracies and CEO of Valens Global. NATHANIEL BARR is the research manager at Valens Global.

The Women Who Escaped ISIS

From Abused to Accused

Letta Tayler

Veiled women sit as they chat in a garden in the northern province of Raqqa, March 31, 2014. ISIS imposed sweeping restrictions on personal freedoms in the northern province of Raqqa. Among the restrictions, Women had to wear the niqab, or full face veil, in public or face unspecified punishments "in accordance with sharia" or Islamic law.

Dressed in fitted slacks, a satin bomber jacket with a fake fur collar, and a black scarf that loosely framed her face, Nadia, 22, spoke in a dull monotone of her journey from life under the Islamic State (also known as ISIS) to life in a Kurdish prison. She said she had not seen her three-year-old daughter since she fled her abusive husband, a fugitive ISIS member, in March.

A Sunni Arab from the Salahuddin Governorate in central Iraq, Nadia—whose name has been changed to protect her identity—was married off to a local farmer in

2012. Although their marriage was arranged, they got along at first, she told me from the visiting room of an Erbil prison. But everything changed for the worse when ISIS took over their village for two months in 2014.

What happened next underscores the serious challenges the Kurdistan Regional Government (KRG) faces as it seeks to identify security threats among the hundreds of thousands of Iraqis streaming across its borders from ISIS-held territory and to prosecute those who were part of the extremist group. During this difficult process, there is a risk that the KRG may be arbitrarily branding many women and even children who lived under ISIS as guilty by association—including those who had not welcomed the extremist group or were abused during its harsh rule.

Many residents fled Nadia's village when ISIS took over. But Nadia said that her husband insisted they remain to care for their cattle. After Iraqi forces routed ISIS a few months later, village elders returned and banished them and others who had not run away, accusing them of being ISIS sympathizers.

Yazidi sisters, who escaped from captivity by Islamic State militants, sit in a tent at Sharya refugee camp on the outskirts of Duhok province, July 3, 2015.

The couple moved with their infant daughter to Mosul, and there her husband, unable to find other work, did join ISIS as a checkpoint guard. Although he initially joined to support his family, said Nadia, he became increasingly "brainwashed" and quickly turned "aggressive," beating her routinely. "He didn't beat me until he joined ISIS," said Nadia. "They changed him, they spoiled his mindset." When she said she would leave him, he threatened to either kill her or take away their daughter.

But when ISIS began pressuring Nadia's husband to become a frontline fighter, he refused—and was beaten and jailed by the group for two months. The day after his release in November 2015, he fled to neighboring Turkey. After ISIS discovered his escape, one of its enforcers tried to make Nadia reveal his whereabouts. When she refused, she said, the enforcer hit her on the head with his rifle and threatened to kill her. Her in-laws feared for her life and persuaded her to let them smuggle her and her daughter into Turkey to join her husband.

She and her daughter reached Turkey after a weeks-long journey involving two sets of smugglers, crossing first into Syria on the back of a truck in a cage hidden beneath bags of sand and soil. "The guards would poke the soil with a stick to see if there was anything beneath it," Nadia said. Terrified her daughter would cry, she said she reluctantly doped her with cold medicine. But she survived that trip only to be battered anew by her husband. "He beat me again and again and again," Nadia told me. When he discovered she was plotting to return to Iraq with their daughter, "he threw me out of the apartment and closed the door in my face," refusing to let her take their daughter with her.

Alone and terrified, she said she crossed the southern Turkish border into what she thought was a sanctuary: Iraqi Kurdistan, whose troops are a key force in the international coalition fighting ISIS. But during a search of the bus she was traveling in, Asayish, the security arm of the KRG, arrested her after finding what they considered to be incriminating photos on her phone. One showed her wearing a black cap with the ISIS logo.

"It was a joke, a terrible joke," Nadia said of the photo, insisting she was not an ISIS member or sympathizer. The photo showed her fully made up with her hair down. "It was an insult to ISIS, as women should cover their faces and not wear makeup," she told me. "If [members of ISIS] had seen this photo, they would have slaughtered me." Another photo showed Nadia's husband sporting a flowing beard and posing with an assault rifle. Nadia said she immediately told the Asayish agents that the photo was of her husband, that he had been an ISIS member, and that she was fleeing him. "Why would I keep that photo of my husband if I wanted to protect him?" she said she asked the agents. They did not believe her.

Now in her 12th month of detention at the Women and Children's Reformatory in Erbil, Nadia is charged with participation in a terrorist group, which carries a sentence of up to 15 years. For the first 17 days of imprisonment, she said, security agents held her in isolation in a dank cell in an unsuccessful attempt to make her confess allegiance to ISIS. Solitary confinement for more than 15 days can constitute inhumane treatment and in some cases torture under United Nations standards. Her cell had no heat. The toilet was broken, and the two tiny windows were located near the ceiling. "They wanted to pressure me [into confessing]," Nadia said. "I wanted to kill myself. I was crying and begging, 'Please, get me out of here.'" For four months, Nadia said, she could not make phone calls or take family visits. When we spoke in December, the KRG had still not provided her with a lawyer, and she said she had seen a judge only once.

AT THE REFORMATORY

Nadia was one of ten women detained on terrorism-related offenses whom I interviewed at the Women and Children's Reformatory. Two of the women had been convicted for trying to commit suicide bombings—one of them in 2008—and readily admitted this was the case. But the other eight women claimed that their only crime was being related by marriage or blood to a member of ISIS or its precursor, al Qaeda in Iraq. Many of the eight women said they had not been provided with a lawyer, as required under Iraqi law. They had spent anywhere from one to nine months in prison without charge or trial. International law requires that detainees be charged "promptly," a period that should not exceed a few days or, at most, a few weeks. Six of the women's children, ranging in age from ten months to eight years, were living inside the prison with them.

Dindar Zebari, the KRG liaison for nongovernmental organizations, denied any abuse of detainees and said that the KRG does its utmost to uphold the rights of the accused. Legal proceedings for terrorism-related cases tend to be more complex and take longer than those for common crimes, he said. Zebari insisted that the photos on Nadia's phone were, in fact, "an indication of [her] support for ISIS." He said a court would provide her and all others accused with lawyers if they could not hire one.

In a positive step for justice, on February 22, an Erbil court dismissed a case against Bassema Darwish, a Yazidi mother of three who had been enslaved and raped by an ISIS emir. The KRG had accused Darwish of complicity in the killings of three KRG peshmerga by ISIS fighters in October 2014. Darwish told the court an Asayish interrogator had beaten her and threatened her with rape if she did not confess to a role in the killings. Still, justice had been slow in coming: Darwish waited 28 months in prison to go to trial. And her case is not yet over: she remains in custody during a 30-day window for the KRG to decide whether to file an appeal and will most likely remain locked up pending the outcome of her case should it do so.

Veiled women walk past a billboard that carries a verse from the Koran urging women to wear a hijab in the northern province of Raqqa, March 31, 2014.

The women and children I met at the Erbil reformatory had frequent access to a large courtyard. But much of the time the mothers and children were crowded into a poorly ventilated cell with the other female prisoners. Prison staff said the cell, housing 24 people, was built for half that number.

One of the prisoners, Yasmine, had been a 16-year-old widow when KRG forces caught her trying to enter Erbil wearing a suicide vest in 2008. Yasmine, who also did not want to disclose her real name, told me that al Qaeda in Iraq had recruited her by barraging her with messages and calls saying that U.S. forces had killed her husband and that she needed to avenge his death. Twenty months have passed since Yasmine completed her seven-year prison term, but she remains in jail. The KRG authorities, she and a family member said, had accused her of developing links to ISIS during her years in detention and would not let her leave prison, even though a judge had ordered her released for lack of evidence.

Among the women awaiting charge or trial, one said she was detained because her son had joined al Qaeda in Iraq a decade earlier, although she had cut off all contact with him since then because he had joined the extremist group. Another woman said that she was related to a prominent ISIS member but had never even spoken with the relative and had seen him only once in her life, at a family gathering in 2002. A third woman said that she and her husband, a former Iraqi police officer, were detained as ISIS suspects because their home was the only one in their village that ISIS had not destroyed; she said that was because ISIS had taken over the house and kicked them out.

Two women said that ISIS had killed one or more of their family members. Three women, including Nadia, said they had left their husbands because the men joined ISIS and that their spouses had threatened and beaten them or taken their children away in retaliation.

Nadia is scheduled to go to trial on April 18. But she is charged under the KRG counterterrorism law of 2006, which lapsed last July, potentially leaving her in a legal limbo, along with many of the 1,500 other Iraqis the KRG says it is holding as ISIS suspects.

As the KRG authorities try to get to the bottom of cases like Nadia's, it's critical that they base their findings on credible evidence and resist assuming guilt by association. The challenge of keeping the region safe from groups such as ISIS is immense, but it does not absolve authorities of the responsibility to afford suspects the due process rights to which they are entitled under domestic and international law.

As a start, the KRG should prioritize impartial investigations into the merits of the accusations against these women and ensure they are afforded full, fair-trial guarantees, including adequate counsel. They should enforce a zero-tolerance policy toward forced confessions or other detainee abuse. Other members of the international coalition fighting ISIS should press the KRG to do so as well; otherwise they risk dirtying their own hands. Settling for anything less risks revictimizing women who have already suffered under ISIS and fuels the ISIS narrative that the KRG and its allies are foes, not friends, of Iraqi Arabs.

LETTA TAYLER is the Senior Terrorism and Counterterrorism Researcher at Human Rights Watch.

© Foreign Affairs

Who Is Narendra Modi?

The Two Sides of India's Prime Minister

Kanchan Chandra

Indian Prime Minister Narendra Modi at the White House, June 2016.

On March 19, a short man in saffron robes and a monk's shaven head was sworn in as chief minister of the Indian state of Uttar Pradesh. UP is India's largest state, with a population larger than that of Russia. It had just held elections for its legislative assembly, and Prime Minister Narendra Modi's Bharatiya Janata Party (BJP) had taken 312 of 403 seats, securing the biggest majority any party had won in the state in four decades. Yogi Adityanath, as the saffron-robed monk is known, was Modi's hand-picked nominee to lead Uttar Pradesh's new government. He is the head priest of a monastic order in northeastern India and an aggressive advocate for Hindu nationalism.

The appointment of a religious leader as the chief of a state government is unprecedented in Indian politics. The BJP has often included members of the Hindu clergy in its mobilization campaigns, but it has generally kept religious figures away from executive positions. (An exception is the Hindu nun Uma Bharti, who is now a cabinet minister in Modi's government and served as chief minister of the state of Madhya Pradesh from 2003 to 2004; unlike Adityanath, Bharti does not head a religious organization.)

Indian newspapers exploded with astonishment when the BJP announced Adityanath's appointment—not only because of his background but also because of the timing of his selection. The elections in Uttar Pradesh were the first state contest since November, when the Modi government demonetized high-value Indian banknotes in an attempt to curb illicit transactions, and the BJP's victory seemed to reflect a popular endorsement of Modi's reforms. Modi himself suggested as much: the election, he said in a speech in Delhi, marked the dawn of a new India, in which citizens would vote to advance development rather than identity-based issues.

Why, then, did Modi choose a chief minister who built his reputation on an extreme form of identity politics? Adityanath founded a Hindu youth group implicated in Hindu-Muslim riots in Gorakhpur and its neighboring districts from 2002 onward (he was personally accused of inciting some of the violence); has led conversion movements in what he calls an attempt to bring non-Hindus "back home"; and has spoken out in support of U.S President Donald Trump's ban on travelers from several Muslim-majority countries, saying that India needs similar restrictions. In short, he represents the fringe of a movement that is itself extreme. Modi has acted as though he hasn't noticed. "Our sole mission [and] motive is development," he declared in a tweet posted after attending Adityanath's swearing-in ceremony.

The mixed signals have thrown observers into a frenzied search for Modi's true political identity. "Is he really a reformer focused on generating the jobs the country needs," an article in Time asked, "or is the language of development, propagated via an unremitting stream of slogans, speeches and tweets by the prime minister and his top officials, actually a cover for Hindutva, an ideology that sees India as a Hindu nation?"

When Modi ran for prime minister in 2014, some commentators thought that he was beginning to moderate his commitment to Hindu nationalism, in line with what the political scientists Lloyd and Susanne Rudolph have called the "centrist equilibrium" of Indian politics. His speech reacting to the BJP's victory in Uttar Pradesh fed the same expectation. In fact, Modi has always been both a reformer and a Hindu nationalist, and this two-dimensional package is the essence of his appeal.

Counting old bank notes in Jammu, November 2016.

REACTION AND REFORM

Consider first Modi's commitment to economic reform. From 2001 to 2014, as chief minister of the state of Gujarat, Modi became known for the so-called Gujarat model of economic growth, which involved cutting red tape, cracking down on corruption, and making land available to the private sector at concessional rates. Since he became prime minister in 2014, Modi has gone further, working not only to streamline but to transform the Indian economy. The most ambitious of his plans is to make India's economy cashless, using the resulting technology to address issues from corruption and clientelism to financial inclusion and social security. One can argue about the content of Modi's reform policies—the Gujarat model, for example, has been criticized for privileging economic growth at the expense of human development, and his policies as prime minister have been criticized for not creating enough jobs. But what is certain is that Modi is committed to reform, and that this commitment is an essential part of his political identity.

Modi's record as a Hindu nationalist has been similarly consistent. He spent his formative years in the service of the Rashtriya Swayamsevak Sangh (National Patriotic Organization, or RSS), an umbrella group that presides over a network of Hindu nationalist affiliates and is the BJP's parent organization. In 1971, at the age of 21, Modi became a pracharak—a member of a bureaucracy of celibate Hindu men working for the RSS. He later entered the BJP as a pracharak on deputation from the RSS. When the senior BJP leader L. K. Advani launched the 1990 Ram Rath Yatra, a cross-country pilgrimage calling for the destruction of a mosque in the north Indian town of Ayodhya and its replacement with a Hindu temple, Modi arranged for the pilgrimage's kick-off in Gujarat.

Modi has always been both a reformer and a Hindu nationalist, and this two-dimensional package is the essence of his appeal.

In 2001, when Modi became Gujarat's chief minister, he was still on deputation from the RSS. The next year, under his government's watch, the worst communal riots that India had seen in at least a decade broke out in the state. More than 1,000 people died—most of them Muslim. (Modi's government was accused of complicity in the riots; in 2012, an investigative body appointed by India's Supreme Court said that it had not found evidence of his involvement.) In the campaign for the parliamentary elections that brought Modi to power in 2014, the BJP continued to exploit religious divisions when it was expedient: in Uttar Pradesh, for example, it capitalized on communal riots in the town of Muzaffarnagar to obtain Hindu votes.

This year's BJP campaign in Uttar Pradesh was as much about championing the rights of Hindus as it was about reform. "If land is given for cemetery in a village, it should also be given for cremation," Modi said at a rally in Fatehpur in mid-February, referring to Muslim and Hindu funerary practices. "If electricity is supplied during Ramadan, it should also be supplied during Diwali. There should not be any discrimination on the basis of religion or caste." That statement was widely interpreted as an appeal to Hindus under the guise of nondiscrimination.

Yogi Adityanath in Lucknow, March 2017.

THE WHOLE PACKAGE

What is new about the BJP's appeals to economic reform and Hindu identity is their simultaneity. The party has previously tended to vacillate between Hindu nationalism and economic reformism, choosing one or the other but not both at the same time. In the 1991 parliamentary elections, for example, the BJP almost doubled its vote share from 11 to 20 percent after running on a Hindu nationalist platform. That was not enough to catapult the party to a winning position, however, so in the years that followed, the BJP started to emphasize good governance and downplay religious identity. Yet the party's ability to expand was still limited: in the 2009 election, it took just 19 percent of the vote. Only in the 2014 elections did Modi's combination of reformism and Hindu nationalism help expand the BJP's vote share to 31 percent.

The package deal works for at least two reasons. First, it allows the BJP to reach a wider following. What is true of voters is also true of the two organizations in which Modi is embedded. Whereas the RSS has a Hindu nationalist agenda, the BJP has plenty of members who do not have a background in the RSS and would prefer to bring the party into the mainstream. Modi has managed to keep both of these constituencies happy. What is more, pursuing nationalism and reformism at the same time offers a kind of insurance: when delivering on reform is difficult, the party can resort to identity-based appeals, and vice-versa. Seen from this perspective, Adityanath's appointment makes perfect sense. It combined Modi's message of development with impeccable Hindu nationalist credentials.

Modi is not the only leader to mix ethnic majoritarianism with economic reform.

Of course, Modi is not the only leader to mix ethnic majoritarianism with economic reform. Trump sailed to power in the United States by combining anti-immigrant cultural policies with anti-globalization economic policies. In France, Marine Le Pen has become a viable presidential candidate by combining anti-immigrant policies with promises of protectionism and tax cuts.

The point of similarity between Modi and these other examples of majoritarian nationalism is that all base their appeal on a two-dimensional package: economics plus identity, rather than either alone. In other ways—their leadership styles, the details of their positions, and the constituencies to which they appeal—these figures differ. Modi, for example, does not oppose economic globalization. The fact that the prime minister's reform policies are not especially nationalist or protectionist—a point of departure from the platforms of figures such as Trump and Le Pen—has encouraged him to turn to questions of pure identity to establish his credentials as a Hindu nationalist.

The trouble is that no matter whether the BJP emphasizes reform or identity, the main losers are India's non-Hindu minorities—especially Muslims. Even when minorities benefit from Modi's reformist policies, his majoritarian positions threaten them by placing them in a position of perpetual insecurity. And given that the lines dividing minorities from majorities are fluid, a democracy that is not safe for some minorities is not safe for any majority.

KANCHAN CHANDRA is a Professor of Politics at New York University and the editor of *Democratic Dynasties: State, Party, and Family in Contemporary Indian Politics.*

© Foreign Affairs

Democracy Is Not Dying

Seeing Through the Doom and Gloom

Thomas Carothers and Richard Youngs

A woman walks to a polling booth in Bangui, Central African Republic, February 14, 2016.

In the West, it is difficult to escape the pessimism that pervades current discussions of global affairs. From Russia's invasion of Crimea and the never-ending crises of the European Union, to the Syrian catastrophe and the rise of the Islamic State (also known as ISIS), the world appears to be tearing at the seams. Meanwhile, democracy itself appears to be unraveling—helped along by resurgent authoritarianism, weakened liberal democratic values, rising populism, and contagious illiberalism.

Democracy has unquestionably lost its global momentum. According to Freedom House, there are only a handful more electoral democracies in the world today than there were at the start of this century. Dozens of newer democracies in the developing world are struggling to put down roots, and many older democracies—including, of course, the United States—are troubled. The theory that democratic transitions naturally move in a positive direction and that established democracies don't tumble backward no longer holds water.

The gloom has become so thick, however, that it obscures reality. A number of politicians, journalists, and analysts are overstating or oversimplifying negative trends and overlooking positive developments. They too easily cast U.S. President Donald Trump's rise, the Brexit vote, and the mainstreaming of populism in many parts of Europe as part of an all-embracing, global counterrevolution against liberal norms. Although the state of democracy around the world is indeed very troubled, it is not uniformly dire, especially outside the West.

IDEALIZING THE PAST AND FOCUSING ON THE NEGATIVE

Today's intensifying apprehension is infused with nostalgia for the 1990s and early 2000s as a period of strong global commitment to liberal norms. Yet even then, illiberal forces were asserting themselves. In 1997, for example, the political commentator Fareed Zakaria famously warned in Foreign Affairs of the "rise of illiberal democracy," arguing that "half of the 'democratizing' countries in the world today are illiberal democracies." Earlier that year, also in Foreign Affairs, one of the authors of this article (Thomas Carothers) gave a sober assessment of the state of global democracy, noting that "there is still sometimes good news on the democracy front . . . but a counter-movement of stagnation and retrenchment is evident."

And even at the height of democracy's third wave at the end of the 1990s, the Middle East remained almost entirely a democracy-free zone, the former Soviet Union was headed much more toward authoritarianism than democracy, and Africa's widely celebrated "new leaders," including Rwanda's Paul Kagame and Uganda's Yoweri Museveni, were antidemocratic strongmen. East Asia also had many well-entrenched dictatorial systems. This is not to deny that serious new challenges to democracy have arisen in recent years. But the current shift away from a supposedly idyllic "liberal moment" in the immediate post–Cold War era is a matter of degree, not kind.

Those who despair the future of democracy tend to focus on a select set of highly visible negative developments—especially the searing failure of the Arab Spring and the rise of illiberal populism in Europe and the United States. Yet in other important regions the picture is different. The Economist Intelligence Unit's Democracy Index scores for Asia and Africa show a modest improvement over the last decade. Indeed, the quality of democracy has improved in places such as Burkina Faso, Gambia, Ghana, Guatemala, the Ivory Coast, Sri Lanka, Tunisia, and Ukraine in spite of the serious problems they have faced. In Latin America, the illiberal populist wave in the early 2000s is receding. Colombia and Nepal have both brokered peace accords with rebel movements, ending decades of civil war, and have seen record numbers of citizens commit to democratic institutions and norms.

The scholars Roberto Foa and Yascha Mounk have usefully warned that "democratic deconsolidation" may be occurring in Western democracies as a result of declines in adherence to core democratic values. But as Harvard University's Pippa Norris has noted, some opinion surveys based on broader data sets reveal that this is not a consistent pattern across Western democracies. Moreover, the current decline is not widely found outside of the West. In Africa and Latin America, public support for core democratic values has remained high and steady over the last decade. The Afrobarometer, for example, shows that over 70 percent of Africans reject nondemocratic forms of democracy. And despite the dispiriting results of the Arab Spring, the World Values Survey shows that support for democracy in the Middle East is on a gradual, upward trajectory.

OVERGENERALIZING POPULISM

After Brexit and the U.S. presidential election, some observers, such as Alfred McCoy writing in The Nation, associated Trump with a number of very different actors who present widely divergent degrees of democratic threat—such as Russian President Vladimir Putin, Dutch politician Geert Wilders, Indian Prime Minister Narendra Modi, Turkish Prime Minister Recep Tayyip Erdogan, and Indonesian former presidential candidate Prabowo Subianto. But not all political parties or persons considered populist harbor equally illiberal or authoritarian tendencies. Nor are all current authoritarian trends necessarily rooted in populism.

Some authoritarian leaders who are labeled as populist may use populist flourishes, such as casting themselves as "men of the people," but they are at most skin-deep populists—meaning they do not represent alternatives to traditional power who gain influence by mobilizing disadvantaged constituencies. Putin, for example, is often referred to by Western journalists as a populist leader. Yet he is a product of Russia's long-standing repressive state apparatus and is profoundly wary of popular mobilization. Similarly, Egyptian President Fattah el-Sisi may employ what The New York Times referred to in 2014 as the speaking style of "a charismatic populist," but he comes straight out of Egypt's traditional power establishment.

That populism has a global reach is yet another exaggeration. The recent talk of a "global populist movement" sheds more heat than light on democracy's travails. After all, populism has not made notable gains in Africa, the Middle East, or Latin America in recent years. Asia, of course, does have Philippine President Rodrigo Duterte, a very clear illiberal populist, as well as India's Modi, whose appeals to Hindu "majoritarianism" have a distinct populist tinge. But on the whole, there is no overarching populist trend in Asia. The "global populist wave" narrative implies that the world is going through a time of dizzying and uncertain change. Yet the most common problem in countries struggling to make democracy work is the entrenchment of corrupt elites who block any substantial change, resulting in the gradual atrophy of democratic norms and institutions.

Further adding to the pessimistic outlook is the tendency to interpret the rise and spread of protests as another sign of a populist epidemic. As the thinking goes, protesters are angry at their politicians, and populism feeds on such anger. In this telling, the spread of protests means the spread of populism. Writing in December 2016, for example, Sam Kim described the Korean protests against President Park Geun-hye as part of the populist wave that produced Brexit and Trump's victory.

Large-scale protests are indeed on the rise around the world. But what is striking about them is that they have mostly sought to toss out corrupt leaders, not anoint populist demagogues. South Korea's recent protests were about better governance and resulted in political parties from across the ideological spectrum coming together to impeach a corrupt president. The most significant protests in Guatemala's recent history led to the ouster of a corrupt president and the start of some serious institutional reforms. The protest movements that have gathered steam in Romania over the past few years have succeeded in making anticorruption a central issue in Romanian politics.

Of course, populist leaders often turn to the streets when their backs are against the wall. During the coup attempt in Turkey last July, for example, Erdogan relied on popular mobilization to help him retain his power. Yet on the whole, the wave of protests around the world is mostly about demands for government accountability. Power holders in many countries are pushing hard against independent civil society, often trying to limit its scope. Negative though this trend is, it is a sign of the wide spread of citizen empowerment as both an idea and an organizing principle.

MISCONSTRUING THE AUTHORITARIAN SURGE

It is certainly true that various authoritarian governments have become more audacious in geopolitical pursuits outside their borders. This includes Russia's invasion of Ukraine, involvement in Syria, and political meddling in the United States and Europe. Other examples include China's sharper edge in the South China Sea, Iran's heightened role in Iraq, Syria, and Yemen, and Saudi Arabia's military involvement in Yemen and Syria. Greater assertiveness by authoritarian powers has many negative implications for the future of global democracy. This does not mean, however, that authoritarianism, as a type of political regime, is succeeding.

Most authoritarian regimes struggle with profound internal challenges and weaknesses. In fact, it is precisely the difficulties authoritarian systems have in delivering goods to their citizens that often spur them to become more assertive outside their borders. Foreign adventurism can help authoritarian leaders distract their own people from their domestic failings. Putin's inability to carry out effective economic and anticorruption reforms, combined with the devastating effect of falling oil prices on the Russian economy, has pushed him to find other ways to maintain his domestic legitimacy. Provocative actions abroad are a natural choice. Although

China has sustained its economic miracle, its visible corruption and slower economic growth in recent years have forced President Xi Jinping to nurture other sources of legitimacy—a tougher foreign policy is one result.

In short, although liberal democracy is facing greater cross-border challenges from authoritarian powers, the central threat is not authoritarianism's success as a political system but rather the instability that such regimes produce.

Undoubtedly, there is much ground for discouragement. The overall state of democracy in the world is much less healthy than predicted during the early years of democracy's third wave. Yet a sense of perspective is needed: the past was not as bright as many seem to remember, democracy is holding steady in some regions, populism is not as global a trend as is often portrayed, and most people are more interested in accountability than illiberalism. The tendency to view global developments through the lens of antidemocratic counterrevolution provides a distorted picture. A more nuanced perspective might not dispel the gloom, but it may help prevent a lapse into disabling pessimism and, consequently, the mistake of giving up on supporting democracy as part of Western foreign policy.

THOMAS CAROTHERS is Senior Vice President for Studies at the Carnegie Endowment for International Peace. His most recent book is *Development Aid Confronts Politics: The Almost Revolution*. RICHARD YOUNGS is a Senior Fellow at the Carnegie Endowment for International Peace. He is the author of eleven books on democracy and European policy, including the new book, *Europe's Eastern Crisis: The Geopolitics of Asymmetry*.

Fake History

How a Nazi Massacre Came to Be Remembered as Its Opposite

Lawrence Douglas

A man takes a picture inside an exhibit on the Nuremberg Trials in Nuremberg, Germany, November 2010.

Bill O'Reilly, late of Fox News, once made the following claim in an exchange with former NATO Supreme Commander Wesley Clark: "In Malmedy, as you know, U.S. forces captured SS forces who had their hands in the air and were unarmed, and they shot them down. You know that. That's on the record. Been documented." Of course, Clark knew nothing of the sort. O'Reilly had gotten the facts completely reversed, and not for the first time—several months earlier, he had made the identical misstatement on air. However astonishing, O'Reilly's false claim was hardly unusual. It offered no more than an extreme example of the bizarre form that the Malmedy affair has assumed in collective memory.

The story of how a massacre of U.S. soldiers came to be remembered as an instance of American abuse of defenseless Nazis is the subject of Steven Remy's rigorously researched new book, The Malmedy Massacre: The War Crimes Trial Controversy. Remy, an associate professor at Brooklyn College and CUNY's Graduate Center, is hardly the first historian to write about the Malmedy affair. But whereas previous histories have largely accepted the myth of U.S. malfeasance, The Malmedy Massacre convincingly corrects the record. In so doing, Remy offers a timely study of the process of historical mythmaking—how false and distorted accounts come to constitute their own durable reality.

THE OTHER NUREMBERG

On December 17, 1944, on the second day of the German counteroffensive in the Ardennes, known as the Battle of the Bulge, a Waffen-SS combat group under the command of Colonel Joachim Peiper captured over 100 American soldiers at the Baugnez crossroads, near the Belgian town of Malmedy. As a fighting force on the eastern front, the Waffen-SS had left a long trail of atrocities that included the mass murder of Jews and Soviet POWs in Belarus. Now deployed in Hitler's last desperate push to forestall defeat, the Waffen-SS sought to spread its trademark terror to the Western Front. Having assembled the captured Americans on a snowy field, members of Peiper's combat group proceeded to mow them down with machine gun fire. All told, 84 GIs were murdered. News of the massacre—the single largest atrocity against American soldiers in the European theater—spread quickly, with Supreme Allied Commander Dwight D. Eisenhower demanding that the SS perpetrators be brought to justice.

After the end of the war, they were. From May to July, 1946, 74 members of combat group Peiper were tried by a U.S. military commission. It was one of hundreds of trials conducted by the Allies in occupied Germany. Most famous among these remains the Nuremberg trial of 22 leading Nazi officials before the International Military Tribunal, which, with its British, French, Soviet, and U.S. judges, was the first international criminal court in history. In the same Nuremberg courtroom, the U.S. military also staged 12 successor trials of nearly 200 leading political, military, and business functionaries of the Nazi state. Finally, on the site of the former Dachau concentration camp, the U.S. army tried over 1,500 Germans, including those responsible for the Malmedy massacre, for violations of the usages and customs of war.

Joachim Peiper and other defendants at trial in 1946.

The Dachau trials have largely faded from public memory. In part, this is because the accused were relatively small fish. The Nuremberg defendants represented major figures, such as Hermann Göring and Hans Frank, who were responsible for crimes against peace, war crimes, and crimes against humanity—spectacular atrocities that stretched over a continent and the span of years. The Dachau trials typically featured German civilians accused of murdering downed American airmen, and lower-level SS men charged with crimes against American soldiers and persons interned in concentration camps liberated by U.S. forces.

As trials conducted by the U.S. army, moreover, the Dachau proceedings were of minor interest to international jurists committed to building on Nuremberg's path-breaking exercise in international criminal law. True, Nuremberg was staged under Allied military auspices, but the tribunal itself featured world-class legal talent largely drawn from the ranks of civilian life. The Dachau courts, by contrast, bore all the traits of standard army military commissions, with guilt determined by a panel consisting of five senior military officers, only one of whom was required to have any legal training.

Military commissions have played a long role in U.S. legal history. As early as 1780, George Washington convened a Board of General Officers to weigh charges of espionage against British Major John André, later executed by order of the commanding general. During the Civil War, as many as 6,000 trials were conducted by military commission. After the war, President Andrew Johnson used one to try the conspirators in the assassination of Abraham Lincoln, presumably out of fear that a civilian jury in Washington, D.C. might have southern sympathies and fail to convict. In 1942, little more than half a year after the United States entered the war in Europe, President Franklin D. Roosevelt hastily convened a military commission to try a handful of Nazi saboteurs who had landed on domestic shores. And in addition to their widespread use in occupied Germany, military commissions were established in both the Philippines and Tokyo to try suspected Japanese war criminals.

Most recently, in the wake of the 9/11 terror attacks, President George W. Bush created a military commission to prosecute suspects held in Guantanamo Bay. In its landmark decision in Hamdan v. Rumsfeld, the Supreme Court declared that Bush's original design was in violation of both the Uniform Code of Military Justice and Common Article of Three of the Geneva Conventions. But the form has survived: a commission revamped during Barack Obama's presidency is presently tasked with trying Khalid Sheikh Mohammed, mastermind of the 9/11 attacks, and Abd al-Rahim al-Nashiri, the architect of the bombing of the USS Cole in October, 2000.

THE DEVIL'S ADVOCATE

The Malmedy trial, officially recorded as U.S. vs. Valentin Bersin et. al, charged 74 members of combat group Peiper not only with the massacre of the 84 American GIs at the Baugnez crossroads, but also with the murder of several hundred additional U.S. soldiers and Belgian civilians in the days that followed. Because military commissions are designed for a narrow range of cases—when, say, martial law has been declared or the crimes committed are incident to acts of the battlefield—they operate in a manner quite different from ordinary civilian courts. At Dachau, evidence typically barred from civilian trials, such as hearsay, was admissible. Convictions did not require unanimity— only a two-thirds majority of the panel of senior officers. All the same, conviction required proof of guilt beyond a reasonable doubt, and the accused enjoyed much the same rights accorded to U.S. soldiers facing court martial.

The prosecution, led by an army lawyer named Burton Ellis, presented a strong case. Several U.S. soldiers had survived the Malmedy massacre, either by fleeing or by playing dead, and were able to testify at the trial. Pre-trial interrogators had also succeeded in using various clever techniques and ruses, such as the staging of mock trials, to extract confessions from the accused. (This was well before the advent of Miranda rules, which require suspects to be informed of their constitutional rights in a custodial setting. In any case, these would not have applied to foreign combatants facing trial before a military commission.) During the trial, the prosecution drew heavily on these highly incriminating statements.

The defense, for its part, sought to challenge the court's jurisdiction, but to no avail. Its other arguments proved no more persuasive. The accused claimed that the captured Americans had tried to flee, and thus were legitimate targets under the law of war. Defense lawyers noted that Francis Lieber, the German-born jurist who had famously advised Lincoln and the Union army on the law of war, had acknowledged that a commander was relieved of the obligation to give quarter in cases in which it was "impossible to cumber himself with prisoners." Some of the accused acknowledged that killings had taken place, but insisted they had not participated personally. A handful claimed that they had been physically mistreated into confessing, but the defense called no medical witnesses to corroborate these claims. Many defendants appealed to superior orders, an appeal that did not constitute a defense proper, but which could be considered in mitigation of punishment.

After three months of trial, the commission returned its verdict. Of the 74 members of Peiper's group, 43, including Peiper himself, were sentenced to death; the rest received lengthy prison terms. There were no acquittals. The evidence against each of the accused was not of equal strength; it was only by relying on a theory of "common design"—the idea that criminal responsibility could be imputed to all members of a criminal organization even in the absence of clear evidence that a specific member had directly participated in every criminal act—that prosecutors succeeded in securing such an astonishing conviction rate and such draconian punishments.

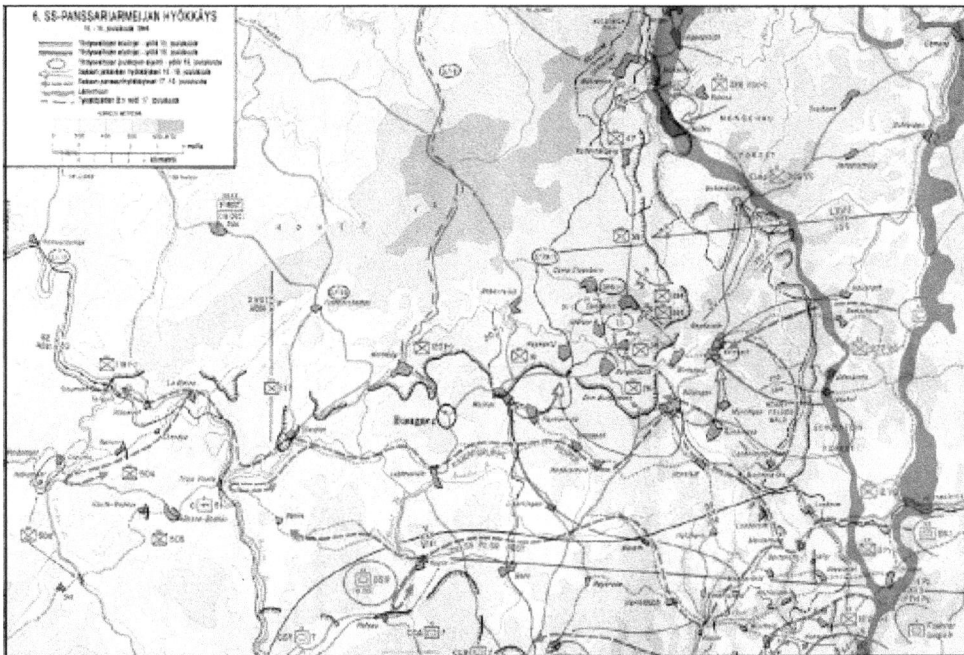

Wikimedia Commons

A map, translated into Finnish, of combat group Peiper's path through Baugnez, where the Malmedy massacre occured.

But no sooner had the convictions been announced than the attacks on the trial began. These were spearheaded by Willis Everett, an Atlanta attorney who had led the Malmedy defense. Certainly the defense had cause for complaint. The theory of common design, pioneered at Nuremberg, struck many observers as tantamount to collective punishment. And some of the ruses used by interrogators to extract confessions might have pushed the envelope of legitimate legal strategies.

Everett, however, blew past the criticisms. Earlier histories have portrayed Everett as a brave and lonely crusader, who, despite some less than savory qualities, labored tirelessly to expose a gross miscarriage of justice. Remy tells a very different story. In Remy's pages, Everett emerges as paranoid, anti-Semitic, and conspiracy-minded. In private correspondence, he refers to the U.S. occupation as a "Jewish occupation" and to a member of the Dachau trial panel as the "Jew law member." He became convinced that SS confessions had been extracted by force not because the record supported this conclusion, but because the interrogators had been German-born Jewish refugees. Although isolated instances of roughness could not be excluded, Everett inflated every allegation such that "what had been a rude gesture...became a threatening move, became physical contact, and finally became mistreatment." And so Everett, in a barrage of furious letters to U.S. War Crimes Branch officials and in petitions challenging the verdict, came to depict SS war criminals as victims of Jewish interrogators bent on vengeance.

In his fury, Everett was not entirely alone. Charles Wennerstrum, the presiding judge in one of the 12 successor cases at Nuremberg, argued that the American trial program had simply convinced the German people that that "they lost the war to tough conquerors." Supreme Court Justice William O. Douglas dismissed the program as an exercise in victor's justice. Chief Justice Harlan Fiske Stone described the international trial at Nuremberg as a "sanctimonious fraud" and as "high-grade lynching party." Everett's allegations of detainee abuse also strongly resonated with politicians such as John Rankin, a prominent House member from Mississippi famous for his racial demagoguery and anti-Semitism.

Once the Malmedy story became about U.S. abuse, it was but one small step to complete the inversion and turn the victims into the murderers at the Baugnez crossroads.

A continent away in Landsberg prison, where the former members of combat group Peiper were serving time or awaiting execution, Everett's agitations came as a godsend. The convicted war criminals joined together in repudiating their earlier confessions, insisting that their statements had been extracted through mistreatment— or worse. Tales of abuse grew ever more extravagant and ghoulish, as prisoners described instances of outright torture: teeth knocked out, fingernails set aflame, testicles crushed. Back home, the Quaker National Council for Prevention of War, a pacifist organization dedicated to American–German reconciliation, credulously picked up and repeated these stories, as did various newspapers and magazines. The Chicago Daily Tribune called for the court martial of the Malmedy prosecutors, and Time magazine described the inventory of alleged abuse as reading like a "record of Nazi atrocities."

The stories fed on themselves. In occupied Germany, the allegations of abuse fueled public opposition to U.S. war crimes trials. Germans had followed the international trial at Nuremberg with polite indulgence, perhaps because they were afraid to register anything in the way of open dissent. But public opinion turned quickly and fiercely against the Nuremberg successor trials and those staged in Dachau. Former Nazis who wanted to avoid prosecution found strong support in the churches, as influential religious figures, such as Protestant clergyman Theophil Wurm and Catholic Archbishop Johannes Neuhäusler, joined the critics of the Allies' "victor's justice." Allegations of detainee abuse also tapped into deep reserves of antisemitism. Many Germans, like Everett himself, came to see U.S. war crimes trials as Jewish revenge rituals.

With sensational stories swirling in the U.S. press and Germans unified in condemning the alleged abuse, the United States launched a series of independent investigations into the allegations, culminating in the creation of a subcommittee of the Senate Arms Services Committee, chaired by Raymond Baldwin, a reliable Republican from Connecticut. After months of hearings, the Baldwin committee issued its sober and carefully prepared report. The claims of systematic mistreatment and torture lacked, it concluded, any basis in fact.

Still, the controversy refused to go away. Wisconsin's young Republican Senator, Joseph McCarthy, insisted that Baldwin had whitewashed evidence of abuse and attacked the U.S. trial program as "communist inspired." Fellow Republican Senator William Langer of North Dakota joined the chorus of denunciation, likening the trials to Stalinist purges. Today it seems inconceivable that members of Congress could hope to score political points by defending persons who had massacred Americans— imagine a senator, outraged by the CIA's waterboarding, seeking the release of Khalid Sheikh Mohammed. But emerging Cold War realities and large German–American constituencies in the Midwest made such grandstanding not just politically feasible but tactically shrewd.

Senator Joseph R. McCarthy in 1954.

In the absence of any real evidence of abuse—indeed, in the face of compelling evidence to the contrary—the calls for commutation and outright amnesty grew in volume. With the outbreak of war in Korea, the United States' need to secure Germany as a reliable military ally trumped any misgivings about the premature release of war criminals. And so the members of combat group Peiper were spared the gallows and even lengthy prison terms. By Christmas 1956, the last of the convicted war criminals, Colonel Peiper, was a free man.

ALTERNATIVE FACTS

The Malmedy Massacre is not without its weaknesses: the writing is at best workmanlike and the narrative has its shortcomings. For instance, Remy offers no explanation for why 74 men stood trial, but only 73 verdicts were announced. (The answer: the prosecution of one of the accused, Marcel Boltz, was suspended when it turned out that Boltz was an Alsatian of French citizenship; Boltz was handed over to the French, who chose not to try him.) And Remy places McCarthy on Baldwin's subcommittee when in fact the Wisconsin senator never actually served as a member but instead had received, as a courtesy, permission from Baldwin to attend the subcommittee's hearings (which McCarthy then exploited to harass and hector witnesses). It is a small but curious mistake for a scholar who knows the case as intimately as Remy does.

All the same, The Malmedy Massacre is a solid account of history that current events have contrived to make exceptionally relevant. Remy could not have researched and written The Malmedy Massacre in anticipation of U.S. President Donald Trump's politics of misinformation, yet he has delivered a sustained exploration into the creation, circulation, and ultimate acceptance of "alternative facts." What makes this story particularly poignant is that Remy is not really telling us anything new. As he makes clear, the record had already been corrected by the Baldwin committee report nearly 70 years ago. What he documents, then, is the tenacity and durability of fake history. To those who subscribe to the pleasing shibboleth that the truth will always come out, Remy has delivered a disturbing counterexample.

Which returns us to O'Reilly. His on-air misstatements represented no more than an ironic confirmation of Remy's account. Once the Malmedy story became about U.S. abuse, it was but one small step to complete the inversion and turn the victims into the murderers at the Baugnez crossroads. When confronted with his mistake, O'Reilly tellingly issued no apology or correction—instead, he simply modified his original claim, while still insisting that defenseless members of the SS had been murdered at the hands of their U.S. captors.

What, then, is the ultimate takeaway from the Malmedy story? Remy rightly observes that the "creation and perpetuation of self-serving myths about the past remains one the most powerful cultural and political forces in the modern world"— though one is left wondering why this should be unique to the modern word. And while his conclusion, that "unchallenged, such myths harden hearts and impede dialog and reconciliation between individuals, communities, and entire nations," makes intuitive sense, it is a claim belied by the story he tells. At least in the case of relations between Germany and the United States, these "self-serving myths" ultimately worked to advance rather than impede the politics of Cold War cooperation. It may be hoped that willful distortions of the historical record inevitably come back to haunt those who craft and peddle such lies, but history, alas, often tells a different story.

LAWRENCE DOUGLAS is James J. Grosfeld Professor of Law, Jurisprudence, and Social Thought at Amherst College.

Is Putin Losing Control of Russia's Conservative Nationalists?

What the Matilda Controversy Reveals About His Rule

Alexander Baunov

MIKHAIL KLIMENTYEV / REUTERS

Russian President Vladimir Putin attends a meeting at the Eastern Economic Forum in Vladivostok, Russia September 2017.

Last month, Russian Orthodox extremists attempted two acts of terror. In the first, they crashed a car loaded with gas canisters into a movie theater in Yekaterinburg on September 4. Then, on September 11, they burned cars near the Moscow office of Konstantin Dobrynin, a liberal former senator. The attacks were motivated by the religious extremists' opposition to Matilda, an upcoming movie by director Alexei Uchitel (who retains Dobrynin as his lawyer) that the protestors have deemed blasphemous. The film tells the story of Czar Nicholas II's premarital love affair with ballerina Matilda Kschessinska. Scheduled for release in October, it has already enraged religious conservatives because the last czar and his family are saints in the

Russian Orthodox Church. On August 31, religious extremists even threw Molotov cocktails at the director's studio in St. Petersburg.

President Vladimir Putin could have easily cracked down on this campaign and reprimanded Natalya Poklonskaya, the parliamentarian from Crimea who instigated it through various media appearances and speeches in the Duma. The fact that he hasn't done so exposes a gaping paradox at the heart of his authoritarian rule.

In recent years, Putin has been happy to inculcate a conservative, nationalist ideology in Russia, which much of the Russian Orthodox Church has supported. And he has encouraged protestors, worshippers, and ordinary Russians to propagate this creed to demonstrate that this is a grassroots movement, not something imposed from the top down by the Kremlin.

By doing so, however, Putin has undermined his own authority. In threatening the makers of an innocuous movie with violence and intimidating members of Russia's cultural elite, the conservative nationalist movement has demonstrated its ugly side, and Putin seems unable to stop it. Doing so would enrage the so-called patriotic part of the political establishment he has emboldened over the last few years.

Up until now, the Kremlin's standard domestic political model has been to lay out a general goal and allow lower levels of society to lead the way there. With the new movie, however, the model has malfunctioned, and the Kremlin is now forced to deal not with one extremist but with a full-blown social phenomenon.

The paradox of the Matilda controversy is that, if he so chose, Putin could halt Poklonskaya in her tracks. But once her grassroots initiative grew large enough for him to notice, it already had the backing of some of his Kremlin allies and associates with whom he does not want to pick a fight. (These include figures such as Bishop Tikhon Shevkunov, Putin's own confessor and an important link between the Church and Russian special services.) The cost of pacifying the anti-Matilda campaign is now sufficiently high that it could mean alienating many of his most ardent supporters.

A central problem of Russia's personality-based regime is that only Putin himself can stop something from happening with certainty. Although his word continues to be taken very seriously, the word of almost any other functionary—even when spoken on the Kremlin's behalf—carries too little weight to stop a nationalist campaign that has already reached critical mass.

A central problem of Russia's personality-based regime is that only Putin himself can stop something from happening with certainty.

Poklonskaya herself has found a particular role in Russia's shifting ideological space. Hailing from Crimea, she was plucked directly from the Ukrainian political milieu by the Putin administration to serve as prosecutor for the region after it was forcibly annexed in 2014. (Poklonskaya was a fervent supporter of the annexation.) Putin's nationalist ideology gained strength following the takeover, and by the time Poklonskaya arrived in Moscow in October 2016 to serve as a deputy in the State Duma, Russia's political center had already spent two more years moving toward embracing Orthodoxy as a collective identity that promised a feeling of superiority over the Cold War's winners. Having found considerable support for her campaign in the Orthodox Church, Poklonskaya asked the Russian general prosecutor's office to investigate both Matilda and its director. Reining in Poklonskaya would mean questioning the country's ideological direction, which Putin is not prepared to do.

NATALIA KOLESNIKOVA / REUTERS

Russian member of parliament and Crimea's former Chief Prosecutor Natalia Poklonskaya attends the opening session of the newly-elected State Duma in Moscow, October 2016.

For every public scolding received from figures they don't regard as authorities, Russia's conservative crusaders can now find public or unspoken support in the circles they respect. That is how to understand Poklonskaya's insolent response to mild criticism from Russian Culture Minister Vladimir Medinsky: "Critical opinions should be given by experts," she said. "I was unaware that Medinsky has a record of expert work." The minister is a nobody, she was saying, and we can find our own authorities to contradict him.

The conservative zealots are also winning the blessing of friendly priests, including the ultraconservative Archpriest Dmitri Smirnov, who claimed that the film was created to mock Russian saints. Fliers attacking Matilda are now lying on candle boxes in parishes across the country. It no longer matters who put them there; all that matters is that they are not being removed.

For these Russian conservatives, Poklonskaya's campaign is a means to prevent the country from sliding into pragmatism. It is a warning shot at a regime that still considers reforms and returning to the club of Western powers to secure investment and economic growth. Poklonskaya is making the point that if a mere film generates such a backlash, apostasy over far more important issues could cost the regime dearly. Putin's conservative nationalist ideology now serves as a reference point for ordinary Russians, but someone like Poklonskaya can embody this set of ideas just as well as he does.

As this new ideology continues to evolve, a temporary, vague alliance is forming between Orthodox priests, security service operatives, businessmen, and government functionaries loyal not so much to Putin as to his declared ideals. Many lower- and mid-level officials are starting to voice support for banning Matilda. And they cannot believe that this campaign could win such momentum without approval from the top. Take the case of Russia's far eastern Kamchatka region. After Medinsky expressed support for Matilda's release, several local distributors still decided not to show the film, calling it their "civic position." The local ministry of culture even displayed the distributors' manifesto on its website. This is a sign of divided loyalty.

Supporters of a free Russia have long dreamed of a day when the Orthodox Church is separate from the state and when elected officials are unafraid to oppose Kremlin ministers. The latter is certainly happening, but among those who are taking advantage of this new freedom first are zealots who speak in a language of aggressive and intimidating conservatism.

ALEXANDER BAUNOV is a Senior Associate at the Carnegie Moscow Center and Editor in Chief of Carnegie.ru.

© Foreign Affairs

China's Return to Strongman Rule

The Meaning of Xi Jinping's Power Grab

Minxin Pei

Watching the party congress on a public screen in Hong Kong, October 2017.

A new era has begun in Chinese politics. On October 24, as the curtain fell on the Chinese Communist Party's 19th National Congress, party officials revised their organization's charter to enshrine a new guiding ideological principle: "Xi Jinping Thought." Few observers know exactly what this doctrine entails—it is an amorphous collection of ideas about maintaining China's one-party state and transforming the country into a global power—but most immediately grasped the political symbolism of its introduction. The party has elevated the Chinese ruler's ideological contributions to the same level as those of Mao Zedong and Deng Xiaoping, the only other CCP leaders whose ideas have been so canonized.

This was only the first inkling that Xi had scored a major political victory at the party congress. The real extent of his triumph became clear the next day, when party officials selected the new members of the Politburo Standing Committee, China's top decision-making body. Xi stacked the seven-member committee with loyalists, all of whom will be too old to stand a chance of taking his place at the next party congress, in 2022. As a result, Xi's rule is now set to last for the next 15 years and perhaps beyond.

Xi will amend the party's charter and China's constitution to legitimize the extension of his power.

However powerful Xi appears to be, he now must earn the political capital to secure an extended term as China's leader. In practice, he will need to deliver on his promises to rebalance and sustain China's economic growth and to restructure its legal system.

JASON LEE / REUTERS

Chinese President Xi Jinping at the Great Hall of the People in Beijing, October 2017.

THE GROWTH OF XI'S POWER

Of the seven members of the CCP's last Standing Committee, only two remain: Xi and his deputy, Premier Li Keqiang. The body's five other members are all new, and four of them are allies of Xi.

Li Zhanshu, the party's new number three, forged a close friendship with Xi more than 30 years ago and was Xi's chief of staff during his first term, which began in 2007. Another loyalist, Zhao Leji, will serve as China's new anticorruption tsar, acting as Xi's top enforcer. The former occupant of that office, Wang Qishan, played a pivotal role in helping Xi purge his rivals and consolidate power during his first term.

Many China watchers have identified two other new figures on the Standing Committee, Wang Huning and Han Zheng, as members of the so-called Shanghai Gang, the elite faction affiliated with former President Jiang Zemin—a line of thinking that places their loyalty to Xi in question. But this assessment is incorrect. Wang has served as the chief ideological adviser to three party bosses—Jiang, Hu Jintao, and Xi—and he is unlikely to risk his ties with Xi by sticking with Jiang's faction, which has been decimated by Xi's anticorruption purge. As for Han, he is a competent, low-key technocrat who lacks an abiding loyalty to the Shanghai Gang. In fact, when Xi was Shanghai's party chief from 2006 to 2007, Han was the city's mayor and Xi's right-hand man. The Standing Committee's seventh member is Wang Yang, a man with ties to the rival Youth League faction. He will become the head of the Chinese People's Political Consultative Conference, an advisory body to the party.

Xi also succeeded in filling the 25-person Politburo with allies. At least 11 of the Politburo's 15 new members belong to Xi's faction. As a result, the president can now count on 18 votes in that body. His decisions will be endorsed overwhelmingly by the Politburo and its Standing Committee, endowing them with extraordinary authority. What is more, Xi's allies in the Politburo, some of them relatively young, will be strong contenders for promotion to the Standing Committee at the 20th National Congress in 2022.

The real resistance to Xi's ambitions will come from China's vast bureaucracy.

The greatest political victory that Xi achieved at the congress was to end the party's practice of formally designating a new leader at least five years ahead of the transfer of power. The tradition began in 1992, when Deng picked Hu as Jiang's successor ten years before Hu took office. In 2007, the party similarly chose Xi as Hu's successor. This practice has reduced the risk of struggles over succession and has helped enforce the party's informal term limits for its top leaders of two stints of five years each. But the party never codified these traditions in its charter, and an incumbent seeking to extend his rule would always have been able to end them with enough raw power.

This was clearly the case for Xi, and he and his allies played their cards brilliantly to break from precedent. First, in the fall of 2016, CCP officials named Xi the party's "core leader," making him the only leader since Deng to have assumed that coveted title on his own and sending a message to other senior figures that Xi's position was unassailable. (Jiang was named core leader by Deng; Hu never received the title.) A few months later, in January of this year, Chinese security agents kidnapped the tycoon Xiao Jianhua from his apartment in the Four Seasons in Hong Kong. The abduction was meant to preempt potential challenges to Xi's plan: as the moneyman for many top Chinese leaders, Xiao likely held incriminating information about some of Xi's rivals.

In July, Xi made another move, ordering the arrest of the Chongqing party chief Sun Zhengcai on charges of corruption. Sun's fall was meaningful because of his association with Jiang's faction and because he is so young that he would have been a plausible successor to Xi had he remained untouched. (Politburo members generally have to be younger than 55 to be eligible for consideration as future successors.) Now that Sun has been purged, there is only one Politburo member young enough to be a possible successor to Xi in 2022: the former Guangdong party chief Hu Chunhua. But the 55-year-old Hu did not get promoted to the Standing Committee, apparently making him ineligible to take Xi's place in 2022. He will likely assume the largely symbolic vice presidency next March.

With so few options, Xi will have the perfect excuse to delay a decision about who should succeed him. His dominance of the Politburo and its Standing Committee will empower him to do just that, securing him a third term in office at the next party congress in 2022.

Xi will amend the party's charter and China's constitution to legitimize the extension of his power. He could, for instance, assume the position of party chairman, restoring that defunct role in the party's charter and restarting the clock on his leadership of the CCP. As for the limit of two terms for China's head of state (an office usually referred to as the "presidency" in English but that properly translates as the "chairmanship"), it could be lifted with a semantic change: officials could revise the Chinese constitution so that Xi's formal title becomes "president." By securing two new five-year terms as head of both party and government, Xi would be able to hold on to power until at least 2032.

The Politburo Standing Committee: Xi Jinping (center), Wang Yang (top left), Li Keqiang (top center), Han Zheng (top right), Zhao Leji (bottom left), Li Zhanshu (bottom center) and Wang Huning (bottom right).

RULE BY LAW

The biggest questions about China's new era surround Xi's agenda. Few expect Xi to become a political reformer, given the crackdowns on civil society and Internet freedom during his first term. Yet optimists believe that Xi's newfound supremacy will grant him a free hand to pursue other changes, introducing pro-market economic reforms and restructuring China's legal system so that it protects property rights and promotes development more effectively.

In fact, little suggests that a new wave of economic reform is in the offing. Xi acquired immense authority during his first term, rolling out an ambitious blueprint in 2013 for overhauling the Chinese economy to, as that plan put it, "[allow] market forces to play a decisive role." Yet even then, he made only modest progress. Thanks to its accommodating monetary policy, Beijing's credit-fueled, investment-driven growth model remained firmly in place, helping to raise China's debt-to-GDP ratio from 215 percent in 2012 to 242 percent in 2016. And although China's heavily indebted state-owned enterprises are a drag on the country's economy, they still occupy a special place in Xi's vision of the future. In July 2016, he argued that the firms should be made "stronger, better, and bigger, without any reservations."

Chinese leaders' confidence in existing policies is another reason observers should temper their hopes for economic reform. Despite the warnings about unsustainable debt producing a financial meltdown, Beijing has not yet paid a real price for sticking to its strategy of supporting growth with injections of credit. Indeed, China's recent economic performance—its GDP will almost certainly expand by more than the official target of 6.5 to 6.7 percent this year—has deepened policymakers' faith in the current model. Finally, because aggressive economic reforms have in the past all been prompted by shocks or crises, observers should discount the probability that Beijing will pursue deep changes when the economy is performing reasonably well, as it is today.

Little suggests that a new wave of economic reform is in the offing.

The most likely political priority for Xi in the immediate future will instead be an overhaul of China's legal system, aimed not at establishing genuine rule of law but at realizing rule by law, under which the state would use the legal system to maintain political, social, and economic control. Should this be the case, regression, not progress, will be the more likely outcome.

There are three signs suggesting that Xi will focus on legal reform. First, the party congress endorsed Xi's plan to overhaul the legal system by establishing a "leading group on comprehensively governing the country according to law," a body that Xi will head. Next, Xi assigned his most trusted ally, Li Zhanshu, to chair the National People's Congress, the country's legislative body, which would draft and pass the laws essential to the realization of Xi's vision. Both of those measures suggest that legal reform will soon receive a good deal of high-level attention. Finally, Xi is a firm believer in China's tradition of rule by law, and the new leading group's focus on "comprehensive" governance reflects that ambition.

To be sure, Xi passed a few major laws aimed at social control during his first term, tightening China's cybersecurity practices and restricting foreign nongovernmental organizations. But much remains to be done to reassert the party's power over society and to provide a solid legal basis for hard authoritarianism. For instance, China could impose additional restrictions on domestic NGOs, introduce new laws on ideological education in colleges and universities, or rewrite criminal laws so that they become even more effective instruments in the suppression of domestic dissent. The goal is to transform China from a decentralized, post-totalitarian regime into a hard authoritarian one ruled by a disciplined Leninist party.

RED TAPE

In the short term, Xi's plans will not encounter much overt resistance. His crackdown on dissent and civil society has been depressingly effective and has eliminated any significant threat to the regime's rule in the near future. Xi's supremacy within the party is now so overwhelming that it is inconceivable that any of his colleagues will dare challenge him.

The real resistance to Xi's ambitions will come from China's vast bureaucracy. Numbering in the millions, the regime's lower and middle officials are first and foremost self-interested human beings, and they care far more about increasing their own privilege and wealth than about promoting abstract ideological goals. As Xi has dismantled the sharing of power and spoils that characterized China's postTiananmen order, these bureaucrats' prospects for money and power have dimmed. No longer are there several elite cliques to join or multiple patrons to serve. Today, every official must compete for favors from a regime dominated by a single faction, and there are fewer paths to advancement than there were before Xi took power. Worse still, Xi's anticorruption crackdown has eliminated the lavish bribes and perks that underwrote bureaucrats' lifestyles for most of the past two decades. Unless Xi relents and allows the regime's rank and file to start feathering their nests again, loyalty will lose its appeal.

To be sure, most lower-level apparatchiks will not abandon the party or display their unhappiness in the open. Instead, they will do what Chinese bureaucrats have done for thousands of years: passively resist edicts from the top. The bureaucrats' goal will be to make Xi appreciate their value and reward them appropriately, perhaps by ending his crackdown on corruption and China's austerity drive. The only way to accomplish this will be through bureaucratic subterfuge aimed at catching Xi's attention by slowing the regime's administrative machinery and stalling China's economic engine. However deep Xi's authority may be, it will erode quickly if the economy slows for more than a few years, and China's bureaucrats know it.

Xi Jinping, Hu Jintao, and Jiang Zemin in Beijing November 2012.

Xi would not be the first all-powerful Chinese leader to face a recalcitrant bureaucracy. Mao confronted a similar challenge in the early 1960s, when he thought that party apparatchiks lacked sufficient ideological fervor. One of his motives for launching the Cultural Revolution was to use mass terror to discipline the bureaucracy and restore its revolutionary spirit.

Yet Xi is no believer in mass movements, and he lacks the charisma of Mao, who could mobilize hundreds of millions of ordinary Chinese people into action. He must instead seek to extend the reach of his power from the level of the Central Committee to China's provinces, cities, and counties. That will be a laborious and time-consuming process, involving, for instance, a major drive to vet and recruit promising apparatchiks at the local level.

Many lower- and middle-level bureaucrats will get on Xi's bandwagon. But as his base expands, it may also sow the seeds of intraparty struggles. Realizing that the next battle for political supremacy will be waged in ten to 15 years, when Xi approaches his own exit from power, his ostensibly loyal followers will be more interested in building up their own power than in implementing Xi's agenda. This is what happened during the Cultural Revolution: after Mao vanquished his rivals, his loyalists, the Lin Biao faction and the Gang of Four, quickly turned on each other out of fear that the other group was positioning itself to succeed the aging chairman.

IN XI'S HANDS

In the years after Mao's death, Chinese leaders came to understand that concentrating power in the hands of a single figure could spell disaster for the party. That is why the survivors of the Cultural Revolution banded together in the 1980s to make sure that a Mao-like leader could never again rule China. The changes ushered in by that group—such as collective leadership, the informal rules regarding succession, and implicit guarantees of security for senior leaders—delivered a level of elite stability unprecedented in the party's history. They also helped the regime avoid making the kinds of dangerous mistakes that can follow from the consolidation of power in a single pair of hands.

Chinese officials seem to have forgotten those lessons. Now that the CCP has returned to strongman rule, its future will depend almost entirely on the quality of Xi's decisions. There will be few constraints on how he makes them. The last time the party had a leader with such unchecked power, the consequences were calamitous. One can only hope that Chinese leaders know what they are doing this time—and that the result will be different.

___

MINXIN PEI is the Tom and Margot Pritzker '72 Professor of Government at Claremont McKenna College and the author of *China's Crony Capitalism*.

www.ingramcontent.com/pod-product-compliance
Lightning Source LLC
Chambersburg PA
CBHW081151270326
41930CB00014B/3115